Abby A. Judson

Why She Became a Spiritualist

Twelve lectures delivered before the Minneapolis Association of Spiritualists

Abby A. Judson

Why She Became a Spiritualist
Twelve lectures delivered before the Minneapolis Association of Spiritualists

ISBN/EAN: 9783337289492

Printed in Europe, USA, Canada, Australia, Japan

Cover: Foto ©Thomas Meinert / pixelio.de

More available books at **www.hansebooks.com**

Why She Became a Spiritualist:

TWELVE LECTURES

Delivered before the

Minneapolis Association of Spiritualists,

BY

ABBY A. JUDSON,

Daughter of ADONIRAM JUDSON, *Missionary to the Burmese Empire.*

November 30, 1890———March 15, 1891.

———

MINNEAPOLIS:
—— *Alfred Roper, Printer.* ——
1891.

THIS BOOK IS

Dedicated

TO MY SPIRIT INFLUENCES,

WHOSE TRANSPARENT MEDIUM I ASPIRE TO BE;

AND ESPECIALLY TO MY

NOBLE FATHER, AND MY LOVING MOTHER.

ABBY A. JUDSON.

CONTENTS.

A SKETCH OF THE AUTHOR'S LIFE.

The following sketch of the author's life is presented, so that all who are interested in Baptist missionary work, and all who have been her pupils since she began to teach, in 1853, may know that it is indeed she who has become a Spiritualist and a worker for the cause of Spiritualism.

Abby A. Judson was born in Maulmain, Burmah, October 31, 1835. Her parents were Dr. Adoniram Judson, and Mrs. Sarah Hall Boardman Judson, both missionaries to what was then called the Burmese Empire.

In 1841, the family took a sea-voyage for their health, and her little brother Henry, tenderly spoken of as "little Henry of Serampore," passed to spirit-life in Serampore, near Calcutta. Early in 1845, her mother's health steadily declining, she accompanied her on a coast voyage to Tavoy and Mergui, the former place being the home of the two missionaries, fondly called Uncle and Aunty Wade, by all the children who knew them. (See page 262).

April 26, 1845, the whole family, except the three little ones, embarked for America. At Port Louis Mrs. Judson penned the affecting stanzas, two of which are quoted on page 91.

On Sept. 1, Mrs. Judson passed to spirit-life in the harbor of St. Helena, and her dear body was interred on that island. On Oct. 15, 1845, Dr. Judson, with his children Abby, Adoniram, and Elnathan, reached Boston. The following year, having married Mrs. Emily C. Judson, he sailed for Burmah, and passed in his turn to the other side of life, April 12, 1850.

Abby was educated at Bradford Academy, Mass.; at the school of Miss Anable, Philadelphia; of Mrs. Hubbard, Hanover, N. H.; of Miss Bucknall, New York City; and of Mrs. Buel, Providence, R. I.

From 1853 to 1854, she was a governess in New York City; from 1856 to 1859, she taught at the Female College in Worcester, Mass.; from 1860 to 1861, at the Seminary in Warren, R. I.; from 1861 to 1864, at Bradford Academy, Mass.; from 1864 to 1868, she was governess in families in Albany, N. Y., and in Fall River, Mass.; from 1868 to 1869, she had a private school in Plymouth, Mass.; and from 1869 to 1876, she taught in the High School in the same place.

After a year of travel in Europe, she taught from 1877 to 1879 in College Hill, Ohio. She then went to Minneapolis, and founded Judson Female Institute, which she carried on from 1879 to 1890. In the autumn of 1887, she became a Spiritualist. In 1890, she disposed of her Seminary, and has since devoted herself somewhat to giving private lessons, but mainly to labor for the cause of Spiritualism.

She used to *try* to be happy. She is now happy, without trying to be so. If her happiness were founded on delusion, it would be unreasonable and foolish. It is founded on solid facts, and it therefore increases with each revolving year.

August 9, 1888, being the centennial of the birth of her father, Adoniram Judson, the event was celebrated at his birth-place in Malden, Mass. Being unable to be present, his daughter Abby, who had become a Spiritualist the year before, but "secretly for fear of" what the world might say, wrote the following letter. It was read at the Celebration, and printed in the Baptist newspapers. The letter is given below, just as it was read, a few words only being omitted, that do not harmonize with the present views of the author:—

To the First Baptist Church in Malden, Mass:

DEAR FRIENDS IN CHRIST.—I wish that the many miles that separate Minneapolis from Malden could be eliminated to-day, and that I could be with you on this centennial of the birth of my father. My heart and soul are with you, and I thank our God that he has put it into your hearts to celebrate this anniversary. Adoniram Judson has been alive one hundred years. Nearly two-thirds of this time he dwelt here in the flesh, and labored with untiring energy for the King of Glory. The remaining years of this century of existence he has dwelt in the land of souls. But he is not idle there. He is not dead. The same spirit of self-sacrifice, the same energy of nature, the same force which made him the pioneer missionary here, the same burning love for his fellow-creatures, the same devotion to the Infinite Source of all being, characterize him there as here, for they formed the essential elements of his nature. Though eternal ages will bring added development, he will always be the individual spirit that we knew him here. And one day, if we are akin to him in aspiration, we shall meet him there. Let us imitate him in all the points in which he resembled the Son of God; and so shall we be welcomed to his ennobling society when God shall call us to his heavenly home. With love to all who are one in the *spirit* of Jesus Christ, I am

Your sister in faith,

ABBY A. JUDSON.

INTRODUCTION.

The following Lectures were given in Minneapolis, Minn., before the Association of Spiritualists, during the twelve weeks extending from Nov. 30, 1890, to Feb. 15, 1891. Speaking in public was somewhat new work to the writer; but, with the effort, came aid from above.

After embracing Spiritualism, Miss Judson was favored by lessons from Dr. H. W. Abbott, who constantly directed his pupils to "follow their impressions." This motto, seemingly so simple, has been the key-note of the efforts of which this book is the result.

After returning from the inspiring Camp-meeting in Clinton, Iowa, in 1890, she "had an impression" to organize a new Association in Minneapolis. This was done, and members of the Associaton contributed their labors and made the addresses for two months. It being difficult for the most of them to continue to speak in public, because this effort interfered with their other spiritualistic work, it was felt that Miss Judson, who was not a healer, nor engaged in special work as a medium, should be the one to assume the burden of giving the addresses. She undertook the work with some trepidation, but relied on the promise of the Spirit-world that they would "fill her mouth."

Having given one lecture, she feared she could not give a second, and had the same experience after giving that one. But, necessity knows no law; and, as time passed on, she found that there was always more to say, and what was undertaken with a tremor, became a pleasure.

As her method of putting herself in condition to receive spiritual aid is very simple as well as effective, she will describe it, hoping it may benefit beginners in similar work.

Sunday's lectures were prepared on Saturday afternoon, and after dinner on Sunday. On these two afternoons, when ready to write, she deadened her door-bell, darkened her study with close curtains, "entered her closet and shut to" the curtain, and there played on her organ in the dark, until she saw beautiful waves of magnetic light, resembling the aurora borealis shimmering over the Arctic sky. She then went to her desk, raised a curtain just enough for her to see to write, and then wrote notes, heads, and sometimes whole sentences, without any conscious effort. The impetus lasted perhaps three-quarters of an hour, when she repeated the process, and two-thirds of the lecture was ready for delivery. It was easy to finish it on Sunday afternoon.

When in accordance with her mother's direction, given Feb. 10, 1891 (see page 263), she began to write out the lectures for publication in this book, she followed the same method. All of these lectures, with one exception, were written in three afternoons each, working from two to three hours each time. Thus, each lecture was wholly written out and prepared for the compositor in six or seven hours.

Those who know the manual labor, besides the

mental work, of writing a book, will see that this work could not have been accomplished so rapidly, without outside aid. The author knows something of literary work, and she declares that she could not possibly have accomplished the work so rapidly and so continuously under ordinary conditions.

Another remarkable thing is that this work did not exhaust her vital forces, as has been the case in her literary labors before becoming a Spiritualist. She will add that during the five months in which the book was written, she has been engaged in teaching at least five forenoons in the week, has taught often in the afternoons, and has held from one to four circles at her home each week, besides presiding at all the Sunday meetings, and generally making the address.

She feels inexpressibly grateful to those spirits who have been educating her thus, during the months in which these lectures have been prepared. See hopes they will continue to work through her, and it is her earnest wish, aim, and resolve, to "follow the impressions" that they may go on giving to her. She is not afraid of being influenced by undeveloped or impure spirits, for the simple reason that she wants to be good, and is willing to be guided.

"In the name of Infinite Good, in which she lives, and moves, and has her being, she beseeches all good, pure, true, and loving spirits to come to her at this time," and forevermore.

LECTURE I.

In answering this question, let us first consult the dictionary.

In Webster's Unabridged, we find three definitions. The first is, "The state of being spiritual." This notion of the meaning of the word rests on the common opinion of English speaking people; and all will admit that if spiritualism be not the state of being spiritual, it is not what it should be.

The second definition is the philosophical one, and first declares that spiritualism is the opposite of materialism. A materialist believes that matter is all that there is, and that spiritual substances do not exist. He thinks that the soul of man is the result of a particular organization of matter in the body. Spiritualism is the opposite of materialism, and is the doctrine that all that exists is spirit or soul. Two philosophers, Berkeley and Fichte, advocated spiritualism in the philosophical sense given in the dictionary. Berkeley believed that the external world consists in impressions made on our minds by Deity; while Fichte claimed that it is a mere educt of the mind. Plato also believed that spirit is the only real existence, and that the external world is but the shadow of eternal realities. He illustrates his famous doctrine of ideas in the following way. He says that while we dwell in this physical world, we may be compared to men sitting in a cave, bound by the feet and neck, so that they cannot move nor look behind them. Back of them, where they cannot see it, is a great light. Behind them, but between them and the great light, is also a raised causeway. On this causeway real objects are passing along. The light behind the causeway throws the shadows of these moving objects in front of the men. They see these shadows; and, as they have never seen anything but shadows of things, they take these shadows for the realities. In this way does Plato explain to us his doctrine that while we are chained in our physical bodies, we see only the shadows, while in the spiritual world are the real things, of which the physical eyes see but the images. So much for the philosophical definition of the word spiritualism.

The third definition given by the dictionary is that which specially applies to what is now known as Modern Spiritualism. According to this, spiritualism consists in frequent communication of intelligence from the world of spirits, by means of physical phenomena, manifested through a person of special susceptibility called a medium.

All these three definitions enter into our conception of the meaning of this word; and, by giving to each its due weight, we have a clear and comprehensive notion of spiritualism as it will be treated in this and the following lectures.

There is no use in denying that a large share of obloquy attaches to those who avow themselves believers in Spiritualism. To declare himself a Spiritualist requires a certain amount of courage. Let us follow the steps of a timid investigator of Spiritualism. Brought up in the church, linked by family ties to those who look on the manifestations as a web of trickery woven to win dollars from fools, or as pure sorcery invented by the father of lies in order to damn souls, these beginners pursue their investigations in silence and in secrecy. So fearful are they that their opposing friends know that they have attended a service, or visited a clairvoyant, that they go under a false name, are heavily veiled or even disguised, in the hope of not being recognized. But, having once begun to investigate these matters, they are unable to stop, until they know for a certainty whether there *be* "intelligent communication between the living and the so-called dead." After a while, it leaks out that these persons have been seen at séances, and that they are becoming interested in Spiritualism. Brought to bay by their opposing friends, and forced to confess, they declare that they are not Spiritualists—that they are only "investigating." They are threatened with social ostracism,

the minister is brought in to tell the shrinking in-
quirers that the whole thing is from Satan himself,
and that their course will probably land them in an
insane asylum, and ultimately plunge them into the
lowest deeps of hell.   Many succumb to the pressure, cease to investigate, and tell Spiritualistic
friends that they have decided to have nothing to do
with Spiritualism.

But some do not give up the quest.   They have
already found so much that is genuine in the mani-
festitations, so sweet has become the thought that
the dear friends in spirit life can return to bless, that
they will not give up Spiritualism.   It begins to be
known that they are Spiritualists.   Friends sigh, and
foes exult.   Acquaintances whisper to each other
that they always thought them somewhat odd, that
there was a streak of insanity in the family, that
they are surely a cross between an idiot and a luna-
tic.   Society looks askance on them, business de-
creases, friends fall off, the church frowns on them,
and at last excludes them.   Does it not indeed require some courage to avow one's self a Spiritualist?

Well, why is Spiritualism regarded by many as a
disgrace to those who profess it?   Let us look again
at the three definitions of the dictionary.

The first one is, "being spiritual."   All will admit
that there is nothing disgraceful here.   The philosophical one is that it is opposed to materialism.

While it is true that the mere money-getter does not respect the idealist, yet the real thinkers, the men who influence others in the long run, have great esteem for those who look beyond the sordid dust into the world of thought and soul.   Give the idealist time, and he will in the end distance the materialist.   To judge a Berkeley, a Fichte, a Plato aright, let a few ages intervene, and then see the halo around their brows.   So, it is not with the philosophical definition of Spiritualism that the element of disgrace comes in.   Though materialism has its day, it will be but a short one; and its opposite, call it idealism, spiritualism, or what you will, will triumph by and by.

It is then to the third definition of Spiritualism that the obloquy attaches.   According to this, it is the frequent communication with those who have left the body, by means of physical phenomena manifested through sensitives, or mediums.   Ah! here is the rub.   The world is willing that we should be spiritual; we may follow the teachings of Plato, Hegel, Fichte, and Berkeley; but, that denizens of the spirit world can communicate with us by means of physical phenomena is intolerable.   This is the feature of Spiritualism that makes us despised and rejected of men.

And yet, the enlightened, pure-minded, aspirational Spiritualist of to-day, not only wishes to be spiritual, not only opposes materialism with heart and soul, not only believes that his soul is immortal, though the carbon, hydrogen, oxygen, and nitrogen of his physical body be decomposed, but he also believes that "there is intelligent communication between the living and the so-called dead."

But, dear friends, in our delight at finding that our dear ones can and do return to bless us, let us remember that Spiritualism embraces far more than this consoling fact.   Let us keep in mind the philosophy that rests on the phenomena, and let us ever remember that the phenomena and the philosophy will not avail to better our condition in spirit life, unless we have begun to be truly spiritual here.

It seems to us that a candid examination of what Spiritualism is, according to so plain and un-ideal a book as the dictionary, has already placed it on a loftier eminence than is occupied by any other religious body of the day.   Let us see.

Is the term Presbyterianism as broad as is Spiritualism?   Presbyterian is derived from the Greek, presbus, an old man, and means a body ruled by elders.   A Presbyterian, judging by his denominational name, is far narrower than a Spiritualist, who derives his name from what many believe to be the all of the universe, matter itself being only a shadow of spirit.   A Baptist assumes that special designation because he claims that only believers should be baptized, and that only immersion of the whole body is a true baptism.   Now compare the name Baptist with the name Spiritualist. Why did the Methodists assume that name? Because they determined that method and system should guide their principles and rule their lives. The name Methodist is less narrow than Presbyterian and Baptist. The Episcopalians get their distinctive name from the Greek word episcopoi, meaning overseers, and their bishops overlook the whole church economy. A term somewhat broader than any of the preceding is that employed by the Congregationalists. Instead of being ruled by elders or bishops, or guided by any set method, their church polity is democratic, and all matters are decided by the vote of the brethren assembled. To be sure, their distinctive cognomen might apply to any body of men, assembled for any object whatever. But, for that matter, the word ecclesiastic itself is derived from a Greek word which meant merely a secular assembly of citizens of a state.

With regard to the Unitarians, that name claims that they reject the unreasonable notion that there can be three infinite beings included in one personality; while the distinctive belief of the Universalists is that salvation will be bestowed on all in the end, and that no soul that emanated from God shall be eternally lost. We are often asked by Unitarians and Universalists why Spiritualists do not coalesce with them, for they say that we believe as they do. In reply to that question so frequently asked, we

say that while Spiritualists do reject three infinite
gods mysteriously combined into one infinite god,
and do believe that no soul in God's universe can be
irrecoverably lost, yet Spiritualists know and proclaim far more than Universalists and Unitarians
would dare to proclaim from their pulpits. We are
pleased to coalesce with all who have the courage
of their real convictions; but we are sorry for the
weakness of those who are secretly Spiritualists,
and yet masquerade in the liberal churches.

"Dare to be right,
Dare to be true."

With regard to the Swedenborgians, they take
their name simply from the name of the man who
made an exposition of the doctrines of Jesus that
comes nearer to Spiritualism than has been done by
the other sects of Christianity.

The Roman Catholics claim to be the true church
of Christ, and the very expression church excludes
those who are not of that distinctive body. The
Greek church, again, is another division of Christendom. The religion we seek is the heritage of the
whole human race, and belongs of right to those
who never heard of Christ just as much as to those
who call themselves his followers. God is the father of all, and all men are brethren.

All the above named are divisions of what is generally called Christianity. But this term, though
broad, is limited as compared to Spiritualism. It is

derived from the name of its founder, Christ, however widely and sadly the sects have strayed from
the precepts really taught by the ideally pure Nazarene.   According to them, none can be called Christians but those who accept him as their head; and,
as but a fraction of the human race·has yet done so,
in nearly two thousand years, Christianity itself is
far too narrow a name for the faith of a Spiritualist.

With regard to other great religions, Judaism is
a faith for the Jews alone, for that race has never
sought to proselyte.   Mohammedanism resembles
Judaism, in adhering to the doctrine of one supreme
God.   And it seems a continuation of Judaism, in
that Mohammed claimed to be the last in a long line
of prophets that were said to begin with Adam. He
made a vast improvement on Judaism, however, in
discarding the bloody rites for propitiating an offended Deity.

Brahminism seemed especially adapted to Hindostan, and has never spread to any extent beyond
that peninsula.   On the other hand, Buddhism, the
great offshoot from Brahminism, has sought to
proselyte.   The doctrines of its founder, the pure
and self-denying Buddha, have spread from one
country to another till it embraces more than one.
fourth of mankind.   As has been pointed out in Sir
Edwin Arnold's "Light of the World," Christianity
itself is really the child of Buddhism; but the child
has surpassed the parent, and what Jesus really

taught reaches the heart of humanity better than
the doctrines of Buddha.

Taoism, one of the three great religions of China,
is the religion of reason, and therefore tallies somewhat with Spiritualism. It is however less warm,
and has not the settled basis of facts to rest upon
that our system possesses.

All these religions have their limitations. These
limitations arise from narrowness of doctrine; from
a servile deference to one man, its founder; or from
race restrictions. Spiritualism, on the other hand,
is utterly comprehensive. It is a cult, or rather a
knowledge, that reaches all men in all conditions, in
all countries, and in all ages of the world. Yes, it
goes beyond this physical world, and embraces in
its divine sway, all spirits out of the body, and all
spirits in all the universe. It is all-embracing, and
everywhere adaptable. In a subsequent lecture, we
shall show that Spiritualism is the corner-stone of all
the religions, and that what is really good in each is
an integral part of Spiritualism. The religion of
our abused Indians was a spiritualism adapted to
their untutored condition. They worshipped, not
idols, but a Great Spirit; and their medicine men
were mediums between the spirit-world and this.
But, as the human race develops, Spiritualism will
develop; for it is in us, and for us, and of us. And
when man reaches in the distant future the highest
development possible in physical conditions, he will
be more truly than ever a Spiritualist.

When we say that Spiritualism is the corner-stone of all religions, we mean that each of those religions, in its beginning, rested on the fact that its founders had some special way of receiving communications from the spirit-world. What is that but Spiritualism? All the doctrines of Modern Spiritualism, all its philosophy, all its religion, rest, in the same manner, on the fact that direct communications on those vital subjects are made to men by the spirit-world. An ordinary man cannot evolve out of his own mind a religion that other men will accept. He must show some sort of credentials that either the Infinite Spirit, or progressed finite spirits, can teach him of the world beyond the grave. All religions have had this in the beginning. Surely Spiritualism, which uproots many of the doctrines of the old religions, must have a similar foundation on which to rest. It must have such a foundation, and it does have such a foundation. And the proofs must be of such a character, that this practical, scientific nineteenth century can find no flaw, and no loop-hole of escape from the conviction that disembodied spirits do communicate with us in the flesh. In by-gone ages, when the laws of nature were not understood so clearly as now, superstition swayed the masses, and ignorance led them to accept the notion of supernatural events. In our day, a supernatural religion is rejected by all who can think independently, and religion itself must, like everything else, rest upon a scientific basis. The age of miracles has gone by. Persons now demand practise, not theory; fact, not faith.

Can Spiritualism stand this test? If it can, this latter part of the nineteenth century will accept it. If it cannot do so, it will be rejected. It will be relegated to the oblivion which it would in that case so richly deserve.

As Spiritualists claim that their facts rest on a scientific basis, and as these facts are considered highly improbable by many, let us for a few moments consider what mental attitude should be maintained towards their claims regarding communion with spirits. We hold that we should treat these alleged facts with the same degree of fairness that we exercise towards other scientific facts. The present century has introduced so many surprising things that we sometimes hear persons remark, "I am prepared to believe anything." Experience has shown that practically no limit may be placed to the use of the forces of nature. Intelligent spiritualists know that what are known as physical phenomena are based on the laws of nature. These laws are applied by scientific, disembodied spirits to the problem of opening intelligent communication between the living and the so-called dead.

Many times in history, people have ridiculed

those who had new ideas. The man who proposed new theories and new methods was denounced as Utopian, unpractical, and foolish.

Towards the end of the fifteenth century, there was one man whom the European world accused of being Utopian to the last degree. He was surely a one-ideaed, unpractical man! He took it into his unbalanced head that people could get to India by sailing west! The notion was held to be absurd in the extreme. To be sure he had investigated, and had many facts at command to support his opinion. But, argued his opposers, of what use are facts that are used to support an impossibility? He went to one royal court after another, and was everywhere a laughing-stock and a bore. Scorned by all, this man Columbus clearly saw a truth, to which all the rest of the world was blind. To the laughing, scornful Old World, he gave a new one, beyond the Atlantic; and he led to the discovery of a new ocean, larger than the Atlantic and the Indian put together. An idealist, a visionary, they called him. An idealist, he conceived that the earth is round; a visionary, he saw regions and seas unknown to Europeans. Now, I put it to you, was the existence of North and South America less a FACT, because the most intelligent persons in Europe, Columbus excepted, did not believe that they existed? Well, like the Europeans of the fifteenth

century, some persons now say that communications from disembodied spirits, through physical
phenomena, are impossible, Utopian, and foolish.
But, facts are stubborn things; and an opinion
that a thing is impossible has no weight whatever,
when that thing is shown to be a fact.

Our skeptical friends may say, "You tell me of
facts. Where are they? Show me a fact, and I
will believe it." Our reply is, "Do as Columbus
did." Scoffers said to him, "You cannot get to
India by sailing west. The thing is impossible."
What did he do? He investigated the regions
beyond. At last he went to Spain, and there
Isabella, a woman, she—"Put up the flag the men
had hauled down." Well, she got him the three
little ships, he sailed west, and discovered America.

In the public square in Genoa, there is a magnificent monument to the persevering and inspired
discoverer. On one side of the square is the
house where he was born. More thrilling than
the sculptured monument even is the simple in-
scription running along the face of the roof,
"Cristofero Columbo, Genevese, scopre America."
"Christopher Columbus, a Genoese, discovered
America." Up to his time, they had only the
Eastern Continent. He gave to the Old World
a New World, never dreamed of before.

Investigate with the same patience, determination, and sagacity that Columbus used, and you

will demonstrate for yourself a *Spirit-world*, whose denizens come to this, and, from their more advanced standpoint, teach us of the vast beyond, to which we are hastening.

Humboldt tells us in his "Kosmos" that Columbus declared that he actually heard a voice that told him to sail west, and he would find the key to a new world. He obeyed the monitions of the wise spirit that instructed him. If he had lived in our day, Columbus would have been a Spiritualist. Aspirational, religious, courageous, he had in his nature the material of which the best Spiritualists are made. And he would have been in good company. Let us never forget that the greatest philosopher of Greece, Socrates, and the noblest American, Abraham Lincoln, were both Spiritualists. Socrates often alluded to his attendant spirit, whose guiding voice he often heard. His absolute confidence in the immortality of the soul seemed strange to those who could infer the separate existence of the soul only by their reason. Socrates, like the modern Spiritualists, enjoyed the certainty of disembodied existence, because, like them, he knew the facts which prove it.

As to our idolized Lincoln, it is well-known that he was a Spiritualist. In some of the great emergencies of the Civil War, he had a medium* at the White House, whom he consulted. The most

* Mrs. Nettie Colburn Maynard, White Plains, N. Y.

elevated spirits guided his conduct, and the Eman-
cipation Proclamation was one of the direct results
of spirit influence.

Many begin to investigate Spiritualism with
bright hopes for the future. But finding that some
who have adopted this belief are vulgar and ignorant people, they become disgusted. Well, my
honest objecting friend, I suppose that Paul, before his conversion, found that many of that new
belief were vulgar and ignorant persons. Paul
was accustomed to the very best Jewish society.
He was polished in his manners and refined in his
tastes. His robes were of the best material, and
worn in a style that bespoke the high-bred gentleman. He noticed that the followers of the Nazarene wore the garb of plain workmen, and that they
spoke and acted in a way that suggested their
lowly origin. Paul was learned in both Jewish
and Greek lore. He had sat at the feet of Gama-
liel, and his logical mind had been drilled in the
best training-school in Palestine. These Galilean
fishermen had had no such advantages. They
could barely read and write. Their leader had
been just a carpenter who supported himself by
his trade, until he began to be a healer and to give
his plain talks to the people. He was a man who
walked all over the country, accompanied by fishermen and men of like station. He had lived
from hand to mouth, and had at last died a most

disgraceful death. Clearly Paul wished to have nothing to do with such gentry. Prison and death for them!

But, a spiriritual manifestation made a wonderful change in the attitude of Paul's mind towards these followers of the executed carpenter. On his way to Damascus, to seize some of these poor wretches who lived there, in mid-day he was blinded by a dazzling light, and he heard a voice that claimed to be the voice of that dead Nazarene, reproving him, and declaring that in future he should be his follower. This "heavenly vision," as Paul called it, this "spiritual manifestation," as we say, proved to Paul that the carpenter Jesus, who had been most certainly killed, was just as certainly alive, SOMEWHERE. This experience showed him the power of the world to come, and he then and there determined to follow this strange being who had proved to him that the so-called dead *can* make intelligent communication to the living. Do we find that this new convert adopted the new faith in secret, and denied fellowship with the poor and ignorant men who also believed in the Nazarene? By no means. When converted, "he strengthened his brethren." His learning, his breeding, his logical mind, his suavity, his eloquence, he brought to bear on the cause he had espoused, and he thus gave a wonderful impetus to the propagation of Christianity.

Let us do the same. If we find that some Spiritualists are coarse and unrefined and ignorant, let us with all the more energy work for the cause that we find to be true, and thus, like Paul, "strengthen our brethren."

Spiritualism embraces all, it comprehends all. God, force, life, infinite spirit, call it what you will, is everywhere, and permeates every individual spirit in the universe. Spiritualism makes spirit the vital power that informs all matter. Without Spiritualism, we would have a dead world, a dead universe. Many deny that they are Spiritualists. But indeed, we are forced to be Spiritualists in reality, if we are alive. And Spiritualism embraces every class of spirits, high or low, embodied or disembodied. There are lofty, seraphic spirits. There are aspirational and loving ones. There are undeveloped, earth-bound ones, both in the body and out of the body. Alas! there are malicious and greedy spirits. There are selfish and hateful ones. All such exist in the universe; in this universe we find ourselves, and in this universe we must live.

What shall we do then? Will it do any good to say, "I will not be a Spiritualist, for I will have nothing to do with Spiritualism?" Offshoots of the Infinite Spirit, destined to continue to be individual spirits forever and ever, there is but one safe path for us to tread. Let us each one, for ourself, aspire to be a good spirit. If that be our true wish, evil or undeveloped spirits cannot harm us, nor drag us down to their level. All spiritual existence is destined by eternal force and law to progress. If we aspire for ourselves, and at the same time, reach down the helping hand to those below us, we aid them to rise, and, in so doing, we further our own advancement. Our disembodied friends who are aspirational know this and practise this, and by imitating their example, we shall become better fitted to join them by and by, when, by the gateway of death, we shall enter the freer life beyond.

TRIUMPH.

" Shout ! for the morning breaks,
   Rosy and clear and bright ;
A glory touches the sleeping lakes ;
   The valleys are bathed in light ;
The great world stirs at last,
   Putting its bonds away !
Out of the shadowy ages past
   Cometh a golden day !
     Echo it, rivers and rills !
      Herald it, steeples and spires !
     Kindle anew on a thousand hills
      Liberty's beacon fires !

A long and dread eclipse
   Has held the world in thrall,
And pressed unto feeble and fainting lips
   The wormwood and the gall ;
But out of the depths, a voice
   Is saying, "Let there be light !"
O waiting souls, behold ! rejoice !
   The mountains are capped with white.
     Echo it, rivers and rills !
      Herald it, steeples and spires !
     Kindle anew on a thousand hills
      Liberty's beacon fires !

They broke the arms of the weak,
   And strengthened the hands that were strong,
Exalted the proud, and humbled the meek,
   And deluged the land with wrong ;
But lo ! in the Coming Age,
   The Beautiful Dawning Day,
Shall deeds of love and mercy engage—
   Haste to prepare the way !
     Echo it, rivers and rills !
      Herald it steeples and spires !
     Kindle anew on a thousand hills
      Liberty's beacon fires !"

MARY F. TUCKER,
Omro, Wisconsin.

LECTURE II.

How shall we best answer this question? For, "What good will it do?" is a question that must be met, in this age, in regard to every new proposition, and every 'ism of this prolific nineteenth century. When the human mind was in its infancy, such questions were not raised, for man had not then begun to inquire into the end and aim of existence.

Let us watch a little child for a moment. Awaking from the deep, refreshing sleep of healthful babyhood, the play impulse seizes him; and under the tuition of Mother Nature, he vigorously uses his limbs, and thus develops his physical powers. Becoming hungry, he asks or seeks for food, and satisfies eagerly his craving for something to fill the aching void. He plays and eats, and when weary he falls asleep, and Nature recuperates the little system for new efforts and new development. To play, to eat, to sleep, fills the round of his unthinking little life. He has no governing purpose, save to follow each impulse as it arises; no end to attain, save to satisfy each desultory desire. His immature brain is not puzzled by the question, "What is the

31

good of all this?" As it was with this little undeveloped child, so was it with the human race in
general, in the earlier stages of its development.

But look at the little fellow by and by, when he
has reached a more advanced stage of life. To ful-
fil a momentary impulse, to satisfy a temporary
physical craving, is not enough for him now. More
thoughtful grown, he asks such questions as "What
am I really living for? What course of action will
help me best to attain my ends? How will it be with
me when I come to die?" He who was once a
thoughtless little boy may turn out a practical philosopher, and inquire with Jeremy Bentham, "What
course of conduct may accomplish the greatest good
to the greatest number?" He may become a deep
religious thinker, and inquire with the exalted and
sublime Jonathan Edwards, "What line of life will
make me most happy, never so many myriads of
ages hence?" Such inquiries into the object of existence beset the human race as they enter more
advanced stages of development.

In earlier ages, man lived at hap-hazard, as it
were. Each man got what he could, made the most
of it for himself and his family, and expected his
neighbor to do the same. Opinions and thoughts
travelled very slowly from one tribe to another.
As life became more settled, and the struggle to
hold his own became less severe, he had more time
to think, and began to theorize. If the theory

sounded well, he was content, whether it could be carried into practice or not.   But in our wonderful age, especially in countries like our own where we are free to carry all reasonable plans into execution, when any scheme is suggested, or any new belief is proposed, the question at once arises, "Is it practicable?"   And if it be practicable, then the questions are, "What good will it do? Will it help the individual man?   Will it help the race?"

In this last decade of the nineteenth century, Spiritualism is forced to the front.   Many are inquiring about its proofs, its claims, and its objects. With its amazing claims and disclosures, Spiritualism must stand or fall according to its relation to the progress of man as a unit, and of man as one of a countless number of human beings.

And, friends, we must settle this question as to the good of Spiritualism, each one for himself.   The time has gone by when men can allow other persons to do their thinking for them, on vital questions of heart and life.   Our ancestors in the last century were taught to find the solution of the most important questions regarding life, both here and hereafter, in the statements made in the Catechism.   At that time it was thought very wicked to question the dicta of the Thirty-nine Articles; and Thomas Paine, a true patriot, a logical thinker, and a devout worshipper of God, was damned from every pulpit in Christendom, because he claimed that reason was

above priestly authority. And the time is fast slip-
ping away into the "dead past" for even members
of "Orthodox" churches, in good and regular standing, to allow their ministers to do their thinking for
them, fortified though those ministers may be by a
book, the last word of which was written nearly two
thousand years ago, and yet claimed by them to con-
tain the very last word that God will ever give to
the human race.

Irrespective of church dogmas and pastoral authority, the vital question for each one of us is,
"What good is Spiritualism?" If Spiritualism is
good for man as an individual, and for the human .
race, it will be accepted, it will universally prevail,
though apprehensive clergy and timid parishioners
fear that it be the veriest exhalation from the lowest
deep of hell, and that those who accept it will be
consigned to a very bad place therein.

Well, dear friends, if we do find ourselves in hell
on leaving the body, we shall be there because we
shall deserve to be there, for our own ill deeds, and
not because the clergy sent us there. And, thanks
to the reasonable information given us by Spiritualism, we shall know that we are not to remain there
forever, but shall in time have an opportunity to
work out of that condition.

We alluded a few minutes ago to Jeremy Bentham and Jonathan Edwards. Living near the same
time, though the English philosopher was but ten

years old when the American metaphysician passed to spirit life, they represent two quite different schools of thought. The underlying principle of Edwards was, "Be good, and you will be happy;" while Bentham virtually said, "Be happy, and then you will be good."

Which was right? My friends, both were right. They only had a little different way of looking at the same thing, and of attaining the same end. Happiness and goodness sprang wedded from the bosom of Infinite Life, and hand in hand will they forever walk. No divorce court can ever sunder the bond that joins them. In this case at least, "What God hath joined together, no man can put asunder." Goodness and happiness grow together on the stem of the tree of life, and their growth is without flaw, without decay, and without end.

Bentham founded the Utilitarian school. Like that of Aristotle, his moral philosophy was for this world alone, and he did not aim to be particularly spiritual or religious. He looked for the greatest happiness for the largest number of persons. Sharp, ringing, and forceful blows did he strike on many an iniquitous though time-sanctioned law of old England. In that field he worked, and most of the improvements in legislation are due to the application of his principle that the best results come to mankind by increasing the individual happiness of as many persons as possible.

Jonathan Edwards, on the other hand, was brought up under the most rigid influences of New England Puritanism. Duty, with him, was Heaven's first law. His piety was deep and pure, his one purpose was to make the very best of the eternal existence vouchsafed to him, his intellect was clear, comprehensive, profound, and strong. Before he was twenty years of age, he had composed for the guidance of his life seventy resolutions, which seem to us the most remarkable exhibition of deep moral character ever manifested by one so young. And yet, though steeped in Puritanism, indoctrinated from infancy with the idea of duty, rigidly held in by the tenets of the old theology, we find that the first of these seventy resolutions is as follows:

"Resolved, that I will do whatsoever I think to be most to the glory of God and my own good, *profit* and *pleasure*, in the whole of my duration, whether now, or never so many myriads of ages hence."

In spite of stern theology, Edwards sought for happiness, because he saw clearly that goodness and happiness were one. A thousand circumstances of life, as well as the broad Atlantic, separated Edwards and Bentham in earth life. Had they met here, doubtless in the eyes of the other, Edwards would have seemed stern, dogmatic, and narrow; and Bentham, worldly, superficial, and insincere. But in spirit life, the walls that might have separated them are prostrate, and their souls can touch each other at many points.

Well, it being conceded that goodness and happiness are what we ought to seek, it remains to be considered how they are to be attained, and whether Spiritualism is in its nature adapted to further these important ends.

The main questions with us as reasonable beings are, "How may we become good, in order that we may be happy?" and "How may we become happy, in order that it may be easy for us to be good?" To answer these, we must find out our true nature, and the possibilities of that nature.

Let us first consider the question of happiness, of which no less a thinker than Pope has said,

"O Happiness, our being's end and aim!"

It seems to us that real happiness depends on a true and complete development of all our powers. Well, what is it to develop anything? Is it not to unfold to greater and yet greater perfection the germ within?

We do not now enquire whence that germ came. The existence of Infinite Being, that permeates every atom of physical space, and every individualized spiritual entity, will form the subject of a subsequent lecture. But to avoid being misunderstood, we simply say in passing that in our opinion David was voicing an exalted spirit of long experience and wide observation in spirit life, when he said, "The fool hath said in his heart there is no God." A foolish thought indeed, and one that better be hid away in silence and secrecy, as a thing to be ashamed of!

The germ of which we speak is within each one of us; and the answer to the first question in *our* catechism is, "Man's chief end is to develop to the utmost the original germ of his being." That germ is an offshoot of infinite life, and has enfolded in it infinite possibilities. These possibilities are not added to it subsequently from the outside world, but they are enfolded in the original germ; for, as George Dana Boardman has felicitously remarked, "You cannot unroll what was not inrolled; you cannot unfold what was not infolded; you cannot develop what was not enveloped." And we will supplement his statement by saying that there are infinite possibilities in each individual entity, because it is originally and perpetually a part of infinite life.

In the process of being, there are two distinct actions: first, the act by which the germ is individualized; and, second, the act of development, by which that germ is gradually, and, in spiritual existences, perpetually unfolded. With regard to the first act, the original separation of that germ from the infinite source, we are not dealing at present. We are now considering the second part of the process, that of development; and our object is to show that unhindered development produces the extreme of happiness.

Enshrined as we are, at present, in our physical bodies, let us give a few moments' thought to physical development. What are its main conditions? Are they not freedom, nutriment, heat, and light? There are other essential features of perfect growth, but as these are the most patent, we will speak specially of them.

All physically organized beings, whether plants or animals, are made chiefly of carbon, hydrogen, oxygen, and nitrogen. With these are combined other elements of matter, according to the constitution of the organism. These elements come to them dissolved in water, or in the atmosphere, and they must be supplied in ample measure to make them grow and live happily. If supplied in scanty measure, they languish; if wholly deprived of them, they die. Abundant nutriment of the sort that is suited to their individuality, they must have.

But nutriment is not enough. A certain amount of heat, conditioned to their kind, is also necessary. And light from the central orb of the physical solar system is needful, and in connection with that solar light comes the magnetic force which plays so important a part in every form of physical existence.

But there is another thing the plant and animal must have, besides nutrition, heat, and light. It must have freedom, in order to make use of the other conditions to good advantage, and arrive at the perfection that was involved in its original germ.

Shut a plant up in a confined alley, where it has but little air and light. The soil is poor and dry. It grows, to be sure, for there is life in it. But it is pale and puny. Transplant it to a meadow, warmed in the sun and refreshed by the breeze, give it moisture, and its life seems renewed. The little plant is now happy, and it becomes a thing of beauty, for its development is unhindered.

It is the same with the bird and the animal. Do you think that your little canary, hatched aud bred in a cage, deprived of freedom, can be the glad, beautiful thing that sports in the groves of the Fortunate Isles of the Atlantic Ocean? You give it enough to eat, you hang its little prison in the sun, and let refreshing zephyrs breathe on it. But there is one thing wanting to the complete and happy development of your little pet. Freedom is wanting. You try to make it happy and the little thing is happy to a degree, for it does not know what freedom is. But its being is undeveloped. It is not the bird it might have been if all the conditions of perfect growth had been supplied, though it is not sad, for it knows no better existence.

Neither did you, my Spiritualist friend, feel sad, twenty-five or thirty years ago, when you were nested in the Methodist, or Baptist, or Presbyterian church. You did not then know what freedom was. So you were contented, though freedom, as well as several other conditions of perfect development, were not supplied to you.

But a sadder thing than a caged canary is a bird who was once free, but who is recaged, either by force, or by its own timidity. If you are afraid, little bird, to come out of your cage, lay aside your fear. Come out, try your wings, and you will find a boundless expanse of light and air that will supply all you need. Timid human soul, come out of your cage too, and you will find that the spirit of Infinite Good will not send you to an everlasting and burning hell, because you try to develop your spiritual powers, with the freedom that he intended you to enjoy when he gave you life. And if force hold you in your cage, poor struggling human soul, and iron circumstances wall you in, remember that after all it is only your body that your tyrants can hold. Chains can bind the body, but not the spirit. Even if the bondage hold you all your earth-life, a time will come when your soul will leave the enswathing clay, and enjoy its heavenly birth-right, perfect freedom, where

"Heaven's long day of bliss will pay
For all God's children suffer here."

But to return from this digression, though a digression growing naturally from the subject, we were saying that the main conditions of physical development were nutrition, freedom, heat, and light. Is it not deducible that mental and spiritual development require analogical conditions? We think so, from the natural relation that exists between the physical and the psychical worlds. Swedenborg points out the correspondences between the two states; Spinoza acutely maintains that the relations between thoughts are precisely the same as the relations between things; and the master idealist of them all, the almost divine Plato, has told us that the physical world is the shadow of the soul world. We shall therefore infer that spiritual entities, whether embodied or disembodied, require for their full development, such nutrition, freedom, heat, and light as will be adapted to the psychic state.

Now, bearing in mind that perfect development is the same as perfect happiness, it remains to show that Spiritualism gives to the soul of man just the elements required for a true and perpetual growth. Developing aright will make us happy; and as happiness and goodness are one, we shall in that process be so very happy that it will be easy for us to be good. In fine, if Spiritualism supply the best conditions for soul growth, it will make us happy and good at the same time; and will be the philosophy, or the religion, or whatever you may choose to call it, for human souls eternally.

Let us see how this is. To begin aright, what is a human being? He is while in the body composed of body, soul, and spirit, to use the language of Paul: he is composed of physical body, spiritual body, and soul, according to the language of many

Spiritualists.   Words are however unimportant, provided we each understand what the other means. Now, we maintain that as the body develops, the mind develops, and the soul as well, under appropriate conditions.   One of the errors of the old theology was the assumption that the physical and the spiritual parts of our composite being are governed by different laws.   Those who accepted the old theology acknowledged the development of the physical body from a germ.   But, in regard to our spiritual part, these theologians claimed a very different process.   They believed that the soul was originally created wholly perfect and good, without attaining this condition by development.   Then this perfect and good soul *fell* from its high estate, and after this, needed to be regenerated, or, in other words, to be *made all over again*.   And their reason for adopting this reversal of the usual and natural and reasonable processes of nature lay in certain declarations made in the sacred writings of an ancient branch of the Semitic race.   To these hampered persons, it seems useless to point out the unreasonableness of their tenets.   "The Bible says so."   That settles it, according to their notion of things, for the Bible is their fetish.   That it was written under spirit influence 1800 to 4000 years ago, that it was written by and for another branch of the human race from our own, that it was handed down by manuscripts copied by nobody knows whom till the middle of the fifteenth century, that it contains contradictions and errors mingled with much that is good, all go for nothing with these credulous adorers of ancient writings. If they can find a passage in proof of their dogma, the dogma must be true. "It is unreasonable," we say to them. "It is a mystery," they reply. "This statement *can't* be true," we tell them. "You'll be damned for doubting it," is their triumphant answer. How is it possible for the soul to develop in reasoning power, when hampered by such fetters?

Spiritualists claim that the spiritual nature is subject to the same laws of development as the physical part of man. We maintain that our trinal nature, physical body, spiritual body, and soul, comes from a germ. This germ, issuing from the fountain of eternal perfection, is essentially and eternally good; and, while dropping whatever it may outgrow, will continue to advance, forever and forever. But, being individualized, no matter how long the process be continued, it will of course never attain to infinite being, from which it came. This application of development from a germ to the spiritual part of man is reasonable and natural. It is worthy therefore of an infinitely reasonable being, whose acts are the expression of those natural laws of which that being is the author.

Now, does Spiritualism help the development of our bodies, of our spirits, and of our souls? If its tendency be in that direction, the system is needed by man, and must be true.   First, then, what is the effect of Spiritualism on the body?

A true and nobly developed Spiritualist reverences his body, because it is the temporary home of his spirit, and the proper growth of his spiritual body depends largely on the condition of the physical. Knowing the interdependence of the two, he follows the laws of health.   But knowing that this perishable part of his being is subordinate to his spirit and soul, he keeps the body under.   The soul is always dominant over the flesh.   The carnal appetites having for their object the nourishment of the body and the propagation of the race, he keeps to their true end.   He does not allow the gratification of these appetites to interfere with the growth of his better part, his immortal nature.

What! a Spiritualist, and eat too much, or eat improper food, because it tastes good!   What! a Spiritualist, and a moderate drinker of alcoholic liquids, that coagulate the brain and impede the expression of his immortal soul!   What! a Spiritualist, and a sensualist, in the married state, or out of it! We have not so learned Spiritualism.

Keep the body healthy, pure, temperate, and magnetic.   Then, whether you are a materializing medium or not, whether you can produce independent slate-writing, or not, you *can* make your temporary, physical body a fit temple for your precious

immortal part; and you *can* become sensitive to the
highest spiritual intelligences.   Being that kind of a
Spiritualist, the physical body will be in harmony
with the happy development of the physical and
spiritual part of that composite being we call
man.

To promote growth of the spirit, the correspondence between the physical and the spiritual world
leads us to infer that the same conditions obtain in
spirit as we pointed out as necessary to ·physical
development; viz., nourishment, freedom, heat, and
light.   If these develop the germ of physically organized bodies to their perfection, may we not expect that analogical conditions will develop soul
germs to the extent possible to that sort of existence?   The only difference will be that as physical
organisms are temporary, they develop to perfection, and then give place to new ones.   But, as the
spirit is immortal, its perfection is not subject to
limitations, and will continue ad infinitum.

Well, what nourishment is suited to the needs of
the soul?

Knowledge will feed the soul and cause it to expand.   How is this knowledge to be attained?   Is
the highest knowledge to come to us from beings
who are hampered by the same physical fetters as
ourselves?   Clearly, the best teachers for us will
be those who were once children of the earth like
ourselves, but who, having been freed from the

flesh, have soared to the natural home of the spirit, the glorious spirit world beyond the oxygen and nitrogen of this terrestrial atmosphere. Brought into contact there with spirits who have long dwelt there, and yet linked to us by near remembrances and ties of love, these freed souls can bring to us the knowledge of the life beyond that will develop our souls aright. Our thoughts will expand, we shall see the true aim of existence, and we shall get glimpses of the ideal beauty, truth, and goodness, which are the eternal realities of the universe. The best that the world knows has come to us from those ideal realms. Drops have come to us from those eternal springs that have vitalized the thought of the world; and if these drops are such, what must the fountain be! Let us open our souls to spiritual refreshment, and let them grow.

But suppose the little plant had nourishment enough, and yet was shut up in a glass box and thus deprived of freedom. It needs room to grow. Do not let us box up our souls, and thus prevent the truths from the spirit world from enlarging our soul nature. Let us drop the shackles of creedal bondage. Let us dare to trust Infinite Love, and Infinite Goodness, and Infinite Knowledge. Let us not allow old prejudices, nor dread of an artificial and wrathful god, to bind our souls in servile chains. Let us cast away fear and mistrust, those shackles of the soul. Did you think that God could be angry

with you, that He needed to be propitiated towards
you? You were misinformed. Believe in beauty,
truth, and goodness. Believe in them, and then
aspire after such a share of them as your nature is
able to appropriate. By and by, when you have
assimilated the present portion, your soul will
have grown, so that you can appropriate yet
more. Thus your soul plant will climb towards
the infinite.

Besides nourishment and freedom, the physical
organism requires heat and light. Is there a heat
and a light appropriate to soul growth?

The warmth that is essential to material organized existence finds its correspondence in the spirit
world in the love that binds all together. Our souls
live because Infinite Being is love. A spirit leans
in love and helpfulness to one who is less developed,
it clings in confiding and appropriating love to one
who is more advanced.

> "Love is the golden chain that binds
> The happy souls above;
> And he's an heir of heaven that finds
> His bosom glow with love."

And is light an essential of soul growth? We do
not believe as the old religionists that God sits on a
throne of light unapproachable and remote. We
know God is infinite life, and that it is everywhere.
But we also know that a soul, embodied or disembodied, which sees immortal realities more clearly,
has a corresponding increase of that light which is

a condition of its development. Some one has beautifully said,

"God dwelleth in a light far beyond human ken,
    Become thyself that light, and thou shalt see him then."

We say, less poetically, but more truthfully, that as we become more beautiful, true, and good, we are not getting any nearer to God, for God was a part of us before, and will always be a part of us; but, as we become more beautiful, true, and good, we are climbing up to that infinite beauty, truth, and goodness, the germ of which was laid in our original individualization. As we see more clearly, as we love more profoundly, we shall approximate the condition which is "most for our own good, pleasure, and profit, whether now, or never so many myriads of ages hence."

FROM "THE SEASONS."

Should fate command me to the farthest verge
Of the green earth, to distant barbarous climes,
Rivers unknown to song; where first the sun
Gilds Indian mountains, or his setting beam
Flames on the Atlantic isles, 'tis nought to me,
Since God is ever present, ever felt,
In the wide waste as in the city full,
And where He vital dwells, there must be joy.

When e'en at last the solemn hour shall come,
And wing my mystic flight to the Spirit-world,
I cheerful will obey; there with new powers,
Will rising wonders sing. Where'er I go,
'Tis universal Love that smiles around,
Sustaining all yon orbs, and all their suns;
From seeming evil still educing good,
And better thence again, and better still,
In *infinite progression*. But I lose
Myself in Him, in light ineffable!
Come, then, expressive silence, muse his praise.

JAMES THOMSON (Altered.)

LECTURE III.

DO SPIRITUALISTS BELIEVE IN GOD?

There are many cultured, refined, and intelligent persons who become interested in the disclosures of Spiritualism, but, being devout both by nature and by education, they are repelled from further investigation by finding that some Spiritualists say that they do not believe in God. When making so sweeping a statement, we could wish that such Spiritualists would explain in what sense they do not believe in God. If they would tell what kind of a God they do not believe in, and not be quite so afraid of a word because of its wrong applications, they would not cast opprobrium on Spiritualists by declaring that they themselves are atheists. They are so afraid of being hampered by church beliefs that the word God has become obnoxious to them. But the most radical persons must acknowledge that there is power and life in the universe. If any prefer to call that power God, we think it is their right to do so. Do not let us claim to be radicals, and then fight about a word. All reasonable beings know that there is *something* that makes the universe go. The dear apostle of "sweetness and light" declared that there is a "power not ourselves that makes for righteousness." If a good Spiritualist wishes to call that something by the name God, why, my dear belligerent radical friend, do you scorn him for so doing? Must we discard a good word, because the so-called Orthodox people attach a wrong conception to that word? Let us rather teach them a higher and larger conception of its meaning, and lead them by sweet attractive power to embrace the light and the glory and the beauty of Spiritualism.

We admit that there are some Spiritualists who are so absorbed in the affairs of this world that the spirit-world to them is precisely like this one. The most progressed spirits seem to them just like themselves. Such men are not aspirational, for they are unconscious of anything beyond them that they aspire to reach. Such Spiritualists may have to linger long in the border-land, after leaving the body. But, thanks to the power that does make for righteousness, they will in time soar to a nobler clime.

Spiritualism embraces all grades of intellectuality; and, within certain well-defined limits, all shades of belief. As in Geology we find that many strata make the rocky surface of the earth, so we find all grades of Spiritualists. Some Spiritualists express themselves by the Indian ghost dance, or by the wild frenzies of negroes in process of conversion. Shakers, who claim that they are the "most radical Spiritualists of the day," practice a monotonous dance that makes them accessible to spirit influences. Others engage in the rapt spiritual converse of a Swedenborg, and the lofty idealism of a Zschokke or a Plato. To the external observer, there does not seem to be much resemblance between these different grades. But something does unite them. Each knows of a power outside of the physical, whose influence he feels. Each believes that spirit is regnant over matter, and that the body is subordinate to the mind. Each seeks to be freed from the bonds of the physical man, and to enter the domain of the spirit. Each knows that outside and beyond the flesh is spirit; and they know of spirit power, because they experience it.

Spiritualists believe in spirit forces. But, do they believe in God? To answer, we must settle the meaning of the two terms in the question,—Spiritualist, and God. We treated of the first in a previous lecture. A Spiritualist is not a Materialist. He knows that there is an immaterial part, that can and will exist without the material body; and, being capable of doing so, will probably continue to exist forever. Let us then examine the second term in the question, and see what is meant by "God," as the word is used by devout Spiritualists.

To begin with, there is a wide difference between the term "God," and the expression "A God," so often in the mouth of church people. Do thinking Spiritualists believe in "a God?" Certainly not. A, the indefinite article, is an adjective. It is placed before singular nouns denoting an individual object, and before collective nouns. Is God either of these, according to any church definition? The idea of infinity being always attached to the word God, we see what an absurdity it is to talk about "A God." Not long ago, we heard a church member say, "I don't believe in a God who will not punish sin forever."

How is God defined in the Westminster Catechism? That famous assembly of divines met at the Abbey, eleven hundred and sixty-three times between 1643 and 1649, for the purpose of formulating into words what people should believe and what they should not believe. A remarkable fact is that at that very time the spirit world was making their first great united effort to communicate with mortals, but thousands of their poor mediums were tortured and murdered as "witches." The Long Parliament issued decrees condemning what they were pleased to call witchcraft, in the same years that they summoned these divines to construct the "Shorter Catechism" and the "Larger Catechism." One of the first problems to be wrestled with was the definition of God. The opening words of the prayer uttered by the youngest divine present were adopted by the convention as their definition of God. "God is a being, infinite, eternal, and unchangeable, in his being, wisdom, power, holiness, justice, goodness, and truth." Time was when this attempt to define the infinite seemed perfect to us. But a larger outlook has shown its imperfections. Fine as it is as an intellectual effort, it still speaks of infinity as "a being." And we doubt the propriety of applying attributes to Infinite Being, though these attributes be said to be illimitable. From our present standpoint, the simpler, but more comprehensive statement, "God is being," is to be preferred.

The word used by the Hebrews to express God is therefore founded on a correct idea. Their word Jehovah is said to include the notion of past, present and future existence; and to be derived from their word "I am," which meant "I always was, I now am, and I always shall be." This is admirable, and illustrates the fact that the great Semitic race believed in Infinite God, while the Aryans adopted the more narrow conception of a personal God. Still the expression "I am," as applied to Infinity, only shows the poverty of language. For, who is I? Is I a person? Impossible, for personality implies limitation. We can speak of *a* person. "Being," a participial noun, derived from the verb to be, as impersonal as the infinitive mode itself, is better adapted to express the conception of a Spiritualist. And when by the word God we really mean infinite being, then as Spiritualists, we do believe in God.

Having alluded to that strikingly individualized branch of the Semitic race, the Hebrews, we will

add that though their word for Infinite Being represents a broad conception, they soon dropped the
— true meaning.   Contradicting the notion expressed
by the original word, they narrowed down the glorious idea of infinity, an idea of course beyond all
space and time.   Instead of that grand ideal, they
began to worship a special personal individuality of
the spirit world.   This tutelar divinity was thought
by them to have selected the Jews out from all
other nations for his special favorites.   Prejudiced
by a blind partiality for them, this Hebrew god took
frightful vengence on their enemies by the weapons
of the Jews.   Sometimes he employed the powers
of nature, and slew thousands by pestilence, or engulfed tribes in a flood of water, because these Gentiles were hurtful to his darling Jews.   As their
tutelar divinity intended that they should have
Canaan for themselves, because it was the most fer-
tile country then known, the original inhabitants,
who had occupied it from the time that Noah's
grandson Canaan went there, must be exterminated.   Bravely did they fight for home and native
land.   But they were slaughtered, men, women
and children.   Even the poor beasts were killed.
And so maniacal was this Hebrew divinity in his
determination to murder the rightful owners of Palestine, that if any Hebrew showed a wish to spare
any Canaanite, he was also to be killed as a rebel.
One king, who tried to save his inherited lands, had

his thumbs and great toes cut off by these Jews.

This cruel deity of the Jews was jealous if his people showed the slightest symptoms of doing homage to the gods of other tribes. From the thick clouds of Mount Sinai in eruption, he was said to have thundered forth, "I, the Lord thy God, am a *jealous* God." This kind of "a God" got angry on occasion, and had to be pacified by the slaughter of thousands of innocent animals, every year. Two poor little lambs, males, without blemish, less than a year old, were put to the knife every day in the year, to keep the god in a friendly state of mind. From the time this daily sacrifice began, about 1491 B. C., till the Romans stopped it when they captured Jerusalem, in 70 A. D., counting out the seventy years captivity, when the poor little innocents had a respite, there were slain in the tabernacle and temple service, the enormous number of 730 lambs a year, and for the whole period, 1,088,-430 lambs. Many more animals, and birds as well, were yearly sacrificed to this Jewish Moloch. And to put the cap-sheaf to these bloody sacrifices, the Jews of a later time, who took Jesus to be the only son of this deity, claimed that none of any nation whatever, whether Jews or Gentiles, could possibly escape an eternal and burning hell, unless this same only son should be killed by having his blood shed. My friends, in such a god as this, the true Spiritualist does not believe.

Still, the strong individuality of a Jew, powerfully expressed by his conception of God, whose worship he so persistently carried on for fifteen hundred years, has kept his race from sinking and merging into other nations.

Though the Jewish nation was politically destroyed nineteen hundred years ago, a Jew to-day is as individual as ever. The sublime egotism that was stamped on the race, when Abraham, under spirit guidance, went to a strange land, to found a great nation, still clings to the character of a Jew. His very narrowness and care for his own interests has kept him alive. Crushed to the wall during the Dark Ages, forbidden to own land and settle down like his neighbors, he was forced to devote his energies to money making. Money and jewels were portable commodities, and were eagerly sought for by these poor exiles from Palestine. That a passion for greed was developed in them was due to the cruelty of nations who claimed to be Christian. Worshipping as deity a Jew from Nazareth, claiming for themselves a Bible, every book in which was written by a Jew, they treated the remnants of the countrymen of Jesus most unjustly and most cruelly. But outrages from the outside world made them cling to one another more closely. A strict adherence to the laws of Moses, in regard to diet and sanitary conditions, kept the Jewish physique at a high point. Wherever the Jew is, an innate force

and vigor brings him to the front.   When restricted
to money making, he does that better than anything
else.   Where these restrictions are lessened, he has
made a noble name, in literature, music, statesmanship, and art.   Three times in the history of the
world has a Jew become the prime minister in what
was at the time the greatest nation of the world.
Joseph, a Hebrew slave, was put at the head of affairs in ancient Egypt, 1500 B. C.   In the sixth century before Christ, Daniel, a captive Jew, was made
prime minister of Babylon.   And in the nineteenth
century after Christ, D'Israeli, a Jew, was twice
made prime minister of Victoria, queen of England
and named by him Empress of India.   The shaping
of the convention of nations at Berlin, in 1878,
proved what a Jew could be in statesmanship, when
freed from the binding chains of the Dark Ages.

But, granting all this greatness and intellectual
force to the Jew, we must yet admit that the pre-
vailing erroneous conception of God came to us
from his nation.   The ancient Hebrews adored a
partial, narrow deity, who was a selfish, jealous, passionate tyrant, enlarged to superhuman dimensions,
and Christendom has adopted the same.   The Jew
feared his god, and tried to placate him by many
bloody sacrifices.   The Christian world has followed
suit, and adopted a god who could be placated towards the works of his own hands, only by the
bloody sacrifice of his nearest relative.

By the way, since coming into the enlarged views of Spiritualism, we have learned to wonder that thinking persons are so careless as to apply the words "he" and "him" to Infinite Being. When we have applied the pronoun "he" to an intelligent entity, what have we done? We have conceived of that entity as being male. By that conception we have excluded the notion of female and of offspring, and if we are speaking of absolute being we have been guilty of the contradiction involved in placing a limitation on the Infinite. Conceiving of God as only father is trying to set bonds to Infinity.

The Roman Christians have done better than this, for they have introduced the mother element. Their attempt is however a crude one. An infinite father (itself a contradiction of terms), a finite mother, a son both finite and infinite, and an infinite holy ghost proceeding from both the father and the son!

Friends, the simplest statements are the nearest to the truth. That the finite cannot comprehend the infinite is self-evident. In treating of what our minds cannot possibly comprehend, let us make the simplest statements, and let us use the simplest words. A multiplicity of notions and words clogs our conceptions. "Infinite being," incomprehensible to the finite mind, and yet bearing the stamp of simple truth!

The original notion of God, entertained by the

Hebrews, of impersonal existence, past, present and future, was inherited from their Semitic ancestors. Moses, who wrote their earliest books, acquired his mental culture among the priests of Egypt. From these priests, he learned how to formulate the innate ideas of his people.

To our mind, the ancient founders of the religion of Egypt were far in advance of modern church belief. They tried to bring before the mind their notion of infinite being as including the active principle, the passive principle, and the result of the blending of the two. By these three separate principles, they expressed to the human mind all existence. These deep and early philosophers had true glimpses into spiritual being. We speak of them as early philosophers, though they themselves claimed to be only the youthful inheritors of the learning of a far more ancient age.

When Solon, "the greatest law-giver that was a poet, and the greatest poet that ever gave laws," visited Egypt, about 600 B. C., he went to learn from their priests. He was astonished by their deep philosophy, and said that the wisest men of Greece were only fit to sit at their feet. These Egyptian priests said that they themselves were but children, and that they had inherited their ideas from the philosophers of Atlantis, a sunken continent that lay under the vast waters west of the Mediterranean. Doubtless these pre-historic wise men of most ancient Atlantis may have been the original holders of those conceptions of the Absolute, which the esoteric priests of Egypt expressed by the three principles: active, passive, and result. In like manner, liberal theologians like Beecher, have sought to idealize the persons of the Trinity, and tried to save themselves and their followers from the absurdity of a personal and yet infinite god, formed by a combination of three and yet infinite persons.

Well, in the lapse of ages, these Egyptian priests sought to make the common people apprehend these three principles, by the special personifications: Osiris, father; Isis, mother; and Horus, son or result. So then the common people of Egypt had three deities; though no doubt the priests, in their esoteric and spiritual circles, held to the worship of infinite being, manifested by the three principles. In process of time, many more deities were added, and a pagan idolatry was the result. The priests themselves deteriorated, and lost the conceptions of the early, pure religion. Infinite being was merged in many limited personalities, and the spiritual became material.

Moses, nine hundred years before Solon, learned in Egyptian lore, developed in spirit communion by forty years of shepherd life in Midian, seized the highest conception of God. His simple and sublime statement is that "In the beginning, God created the heaven and the earth." He conceived

of God as spirit, and in successive visions he saw
light take the place of darkness, and order supplant
chaos. Coming to the beginning of man, Moses
conceives of God as saying, "Let *us* make man in
our image," thus recalling the Egyptian idea of
male, female, and offspring. Thus did he make the
three principles preside at the beginning of the material creation. But the sublime conception of
Moses, inherited from Semitic ancestry, and formulated by Egyptian teachers, degenerated with the
later Jews into the wrathful conception delineated in
the former part of this lecture.

Fifteen hundred years later, another Jew, less
sublime but more spiritual than Moses, tried to
bring his nation out of the depths of formality and
blasphemy, to which they had degraded. This new
seer announced the clear statement that "God is a
spirit, and that they that worship him must worship
him in spirit and in truth." Allowing for the poverty and the consequent limitations of language,
Jesus of Nazareth certainly taught the spirituality
of God, and a spiritual religion, compelling truth
from its followers. Well would it have been for
the world if the Christian church in ages since had
really accepted and lived by his pure and simple
teachings!

The formal Pharisees of that day hated the precepts of the Galilean seer, while the materialistic
Sadducees hated his doctrines. In our day, church

Pharisees and materialistic sceptics hate the spiritual teachings that are the legitimate outcome of the precepts and the life of Jesus of Nazareth. We distinctly make the claim that the persons in this age who best comprehend and best follow the real teachings of the Nazarene are pure and progressive Spiritualists. We do not now speak of gross, sensual, money-grasping Spiritualists, for they take the name and not the substance of true Spiritualism.

Do true and progressive Spiritualists believe in God? They do believe in God. They do more. They know God, for they know that infinite life permeates every atom of matter, every organized physical being, whether plant or animal, as well as every individual, spiritual entity. Infinite life, infinite being ever creates new forms, and develops already existing forms into higher states of advancement.

Some constantly reiterate the formula, "God is good." They claim that God was named from his goodness, because god and good are spelled alike in Anglo-Saxon. But the words do not correspond in any other language. It is also unphilosophical to impute an attribute to infinity, thus excluding the opposite. "God is life" is better than "God is good." Life acts. Infinite life is progressive, for such is its inherent nature, not its attribute. Infinite life progresses forever. We may call it by the name God, if we so choose.

Need we fear God? Do we fear life? Certainly not. It is death, not life, that we fear. In infinite life, we live, and move, and have our own finite being. We love the enthusiastic expression of Sir Thomas Browne, "Ready to be anything, in the ecstasy of being ever." During two centuries of what we call time, he has rejoiced in the freedom of disembodied existence.

Life is positive. Death is negative. Life progresses and becomes better. What was good in bygone ages is bad now. What we call good will be thought evil after we attain a more advanced state. Life is good, but the goodness is only comparative, not absolute.

Death stops improvement. It is negative. Goethe had a true thought when he made Mephistopheles acknowledge that he is the spirit that denies. He is not inherently evil, but he represents a condition in which good is undeveloped and remains negative, because life does not urge it to progression. When we speak of death here, of course we do not mean the death of the body, which only frees the spirit to go into a more glorious life. We mean simply the absence of life. Death is not God. God is life.

How can we, finite beings, hampered by this physical frame, get a glimpse of infinite life? Can we get it by looking through the two optical instruments we call our eyes at the physical objects of terrestrial creation? They bespeak a creative power to be sure. But looking at them is not looking at God. God is spirit, or the life that made and informs all physical objects. To get a glimpse of infinite spirit, we must look at the spirit that comes within our observation. What spirit is that? Assuredly our own spirit. Then, to get a glimpse of infinite spirit, we must look within. Let us study our own spirit, and then we see a finite portion of the infinite spirit, whose child we are.

This looking within to examine the working of one's own spirit is not easy at first. We must separate ourselves from the eternal world. In darkness, in quiet, in seclusion, we look within. We learn how active the mind is, we find that we can distinguish the mind from what the mind does, and we become conscious of the strange fact that it is the mind that examines its own self. David meant this when he said, "Commune with your own heart upon your bed and be still." The darkness and quiet of night, the absolute seclusion created by being awake when others sleep, brought to him favorable conditions for mental study. Such mental introspection gives stronger proof of the independent existence of the mind than can be realized by those who live wholly in the outside world. The consciousness we gain of our own spirit existence aids us to realize the glorious fact of disembodied spirit existence, and prepares the way for getting some faint notion of infinite existence. Instead of adoring a material God, as those unconsciously do who do not know spirit, we begin to worship the infinite spirit, "in spirit and in truth."

Having perceived the finite spirit within ourselves, we endeavor to expand that conception to infinity, and we realize that we cannot see God; in fact, that we shall never see God. Does that make us fear? Is the little fish afraid, because it does not see, and never will see the whole of the great ocean in which it lives?

Are we a part of God? Most certainly; for God is life, and we are alive. How are we alive? By God living in us. As a drop is a part of the ocean, and just as truly water as the ocean itself, so each of us is an individualized drop of life in the ocean of infinite life? Need we fear that life? No! A thousand times no! Unspeakably happy are we that life is forevermore, and that we are a part of it.

Infinite life, infinite being, is expressed by laws. A law is defined as "life in movement." In other words, life in movement progresses according to law. It moves just right, and so the normal way of doing a thing is the beautiful way of doing it. To extend and intensify our own share of life,—physical, mental, and spiritual,—we must study those laws, and adapt our actions and our mode of existence to them. So doing, we have nothing whatever to fear, we have everything to trust, and are the happiest persons that walk the earth.

Our so-called Orthodox friends may say, "How can you dare to be happy, unless you have accepted the sacrifice of Christ, and know that your sins have been washed away in the blood of Jesus?"

My friends, I know whereof I speak. I once believed in the limited, partial, wrathful, and unreasonable god of the old orthodoxy. I thought my nature was corrupt, that there was no good thing in me, that my corrupt nature was inherent in me, and that I had intensified it by millions of wrong thoughts, words, and deeds, and that my only hope was in having Jesus bear my sins, and save me by his blood. Even after I was convinced of the phenomena of Spiritualism, the old notions would recur, and make me wonder if I were on a sure foundation. I shall never forget the quiet hour when all alone, so far as mortals are concerned, but surrounded by invisible influences, the mists were wholly rolled away. All false foundations, man made, but esteemed because long adopted, crumbled away, and my soul found the unchangeable rock on which to build for eternal existence. These truths came clearly to my mind. "I am alive, because of infinite life. I came out from that infinite fount of life. That infinite life moves by law. If I do not seek to find out those laws, and adapt my doings to them, it will not be well for me, I shall not get on. If I try to live by those laws of physical and spiritual life, I must be safe, and I must get on. Infinite life loves; in other words, it desires all its creations to progress. I surely want to be good. That desire will draw aid from above. And what is true of me, is true of all." These considerations rest on no Bible, on no Savior. They apply to all men, of all nationalities, of all religions. They rest on the laws of being, and are to be depended on. This glorious knowledge removes all doubts, all fears. We float in an ocean of infinite life and infinite love. God is life. God is love. For love is life. God, love, life, the same, and infinite forevermore!

"Mortals that would follow me,
Love Virtue; she alone is free.
She can teach you how to climb
Far above yon sphery chime;
Or, if Virtue feeble were,
Heaven itself would stoop to her."

FROM POPE'S "ESSAY ON MAN."

" All are but parts of one stupendous whole,
Whose body Nature is, and God the soul;
That changed through all, and yet in all the same,
Great in the earth, as in the ethereal frame,
Warms in the sun, refreshes in the breeze,
Glows in the stars, and blossoms in the trees,
Lives through all life, extends through all extent,
Spreads undivided, operates unspent,
Breathes in our soul, informs our mortal part,
As full, as perfect, in a hair as heart,
As full, as perfect, in poor man that mourns
As the rapt seraph that adores and burns:
To him, no high, no low, no great, no small:
He fills, He bounds, connects, and equals all."

LECTURE IV.

PERSONAL EVIDENCES OF SPIRITUALISM.

Before taking up the personal evidence that laid the foundation of Spiritualism for my own mind, let us first get a clear notion of the system, of which the phenomena form the evidence.

First, then, what is a Spiritualist? We will answer in two ways, negatively and positively. A Spiritualist is not a materialist. A materialist denies that spirit can exist independently of the body. He thinks that when our body dies, we exist no longer. Neither is a Spiritualist an agnostic. An agnostic knows nothing beyond physical existence, while a true Spiritualist knows of spirit existence even more surely than he knows physical and material facts. A Spiritualist does more than think or believe. He *knows* that life is continuous after the dissolution of the physical body. In short, the evidence proving Spiritualism will prove three things: first, that the soul can exist and manifest itself without being in an organized form of matter heavier than the air; second, that life does not cease with the death of our present material bodies; and third, that there is intelligent communication between the living and the so-called dead. If these three points can be proved to my mind, I must be a Spiritualist; if they can be proved to yours, you must be a Spiritualist, unless you prefer to be the thrall of prejudice.

But, what is evidence? What is proof? And how far can they have weight in questions like these? We prove material existences and acts by material proofs; while in regard to intellectual or moral facts, we depend more on what is called evidence. Still, legally speaking, all proofs and testimony, taken together, form evidence. And so the object of the present lecture is to give some of the things that were evidence to me that Spiritualism is true. And I hope that the proofs I shall adduce will make it evident to your mind that I at least have good reason for being a Spiritualist, even though the evidence be not of such a character as to force you to be one yourself.

Some may say that if the evidence be strong enough, it will be sure to convince all; and, conversely, if others be not convinced, the cause is to be found in the defective nature of the evidence. But this is not always so. Many may hear absolute proofs that an act has been committed, and yet go away from court doubting the same. Absolute proof does not convince all minds. Some minds are so constituted by nature that they do not readily accept the testimony of another. Like Montaigne, they naturally antagonize every proposition that is

brought before them.   This original bias of mind
has strengthened with years, until their scepticism
has become abnormal, and incapable of receiving a
newly presented truth.   Their early teachers did
not study the mind that they attempted to guide,
and the original twist in the tender sapling has become an enormous and gnarly projection that pre-
vents normal development.   How carefully should
we train a forming mind to judge things fairly,
openly, and without prejudice!

When a case is to be tried in open court, how
careful are the parties concerned to secure an un-
biased jury!   If a man has already formed an opinion on the subject, we think he is not fit to sit in the
jury-box.   He is challenged, and in important cases
sometimes days are spent in finding twelve men
who are at all fit to weigh the truth, and nothing
but the truth.   A biased juryman is incapable of
deciding aright on evidence.   Prejudice, from pre,
before, and judicare, to judge, blinds him, for he
has made up his mind beforehand.

Many persons are prejudiced against Spiritualism, and therefore judge it before getting evidence
in regard to it.   This is unjust to those who are
Spiritualists; and it is also unfair towards themselves, for they miss a great light and a great good.
Hume would not accept a miracle on any evidence
whatever, and said that the testimony of every living person in the world could not convince him of

a miracle. We Spiritualists do not blame Hume
for refusing to accept a violation of the laws of
Nature. But when we bring testimony regarding
facts that are in exact accordance with the laws of
nature, now better understood than in the time of
Hume, we do ask for an unprejudiced consideration of that testimony. But persons that make
their judgment of Spiritualism without any evidence
at all have put their minds in a poor condition for
judging clearly. There is but little use in bringing
evidence to them, for "There are none as blind as
those who will not see." Still, we hope that grains
of truth will little by little work into the joints of
their armor, for the light becomes clearer with each
revolving year. When the world is bathed in sun-
light, we pity the few who hide in a damp dark hole
in the trunk of an old moss-grown tree. There is
plenty of light for all. Let us all enjoy it!

With deep interest in all, I yet bring my evidence
mostly for unprejudiced minds, because such are
the only ones that are fit to judge aright on any
question.

To be sure, there are some fair-minded persons
who judge fairly on subjects connected with this
present life, but who in regard to Spiritualism will
not allow evidence that would be taken as convincing proof on other questions. They are so
constituted, or so educated, that it seems to them
quite impossible that disembodied spirits can com-

municate with us in the flesh.   To such I will say
that the seeming impossibility of any new thing is
quite powerless, if that seemingly impossible thing
be shown to be an actuality.   A fact is a very stubborn thing, and I beg them to give their close and
their candid attention to some of the facts I am
about to relate, which came to my own mind as
convincing proofs that Spiritualism is not a delusion,
but a substantial truth.

To premise, up to the autumn of 1887, I was as
prejudiced against what is called Spiritualism as
most members of orthodox churches.   I was also
very much afraid of it.   I thought most of it was
fraud and humbug; and that if there were any outside spiritual agency in it, it was Satan himself, or
his emissaries.   Still, one thing allied to it, I knew
to be true.   I was aware that under certain conditions, our minds can impress each other, though our
bodies be widely separated.   Two personal experiences had made me know this to be true.

In 1854, I was governess in a family in New
York City.   My step-mother was in Hamilton,
thirty miles west of Utica, N. Y.   On the 31st of
May, about ten o'clock p. m., I lay in bed, when I
was startled by a white form bending over me.   This
occurred several times, and I became so frightened
that I went to another room, and saw no more.
My step-mother, Mrs. Emily C. Judson, passed into spirit-life the next morning.   I was summoned

by telegram to the funeral.   I did not mention what
I had seen, but I learned from her sister that, at the
hour above named, my step-mother lay unconscious.   I knew her spirit came to me, and I supposed her loving anxiety for me led her to me.   I
have since learned that her spirit guides brought
her to me, in order to gain from me some magnetic
force that aided her spirit to free smoothly from the
worn physical body.

In 1864, and somewhat later, I had three successive experiences with an invalid relative, who is exceedingly endeared to me.   Though separated
forty or several hundred miles, at each access of
painful suffering on the part of this dear one, I
spent a night of agony on his behalf.   The coinci-
dence of time was exact in each case; so that on the
third occurrence, I awaited a letter with certain
foreknowledge.   The expected letter came, and the
third seizure was at the time I suffered with him,
though he was near Boston, Mass., and I in Skane-
ateles, N. Y.

Thus was I shown that mind does impress mind,
though widely separated.   But I had the odd notion that it was only embodied souls, only those
that we call the living, that could thus do.   It never
once occurred to me that disembodied souls could
come to us and influence us.   To me, the disembodied spirit seemed farther away than the central
sun of the starry universe.   This odd opinion of

mine was due to my being really, though unconsciously, tinged with materialism.   I had an indefinite theory that while we are *here*, a magnetism, or
something, was projected from the body, that could
affect certain sympathetic minds.   But when a person was dead, I supposed he was completely carried off.   All that power of projection was then
lost, for I supposed it depended wholly on the body.
When persons died, they went to either heaven or
hell, and there was nothing more of them here.
From my present standpoint, that state of mind was
incipient materialism.

As time passed on, I began to be sceptical as to
the continuance of life at all, after the death of the
body.   The imperfect condition of the mind in in-
fants, its weakness in illness, its apparent paralysis
in cases of injury to the brain substance, the demo-
lition of the mind in insanity, and its decay in extreme old age,––all these circumstances pointed
with fatal finger to the dread conclusion that the
mind depends for individual existence on the body,
is produced with the body, is developed as the body
develops, decays as the body decays, and––dies
when the body dies.   Materialism was no longer
incipient; it was well developed.   Its subtle poison,
everywhere pervasive, planted a sting in every joy.
It also made me, of course with the best of motives,
hide my real views of existence from nearly all.
Very rarely, I hinted these desolate forebodings to

some thoughtful soul. If the person were strictly religious, I saw the painful chill that my words imparted. If the friend were sceptical like myself, it was but sorry comfort to find that another soul was plunged in the same slough of uncertainty that engulfed me.

But I kept these painful feelings mostly to myself. A teacher, and therefore thrown much with the young, I was very careful not to say a single word that would deaden their faith in a life to come. To them, I spoke of God's love, of the perfection of the character of Jesus, of the truths of the Bible, of the influence of Christianity. Thus did I try to water the soil of other hearts, while my own heart was a desert, parched and perishing for the *water* of *life*. I should have thought it very wrong to sap belief in other minds, especially in the young, though I could not believe myself. Thus my double life went on. Outside, devotion to church and missionary enterprises; inside, a gulf of uncertainty opening into a sea of despair.

For, alas! the religion taught in my church did not make me long for immortality. Supposing the mind did continue to exist after the death of the body, what comfort could I take in being "saved" myself, when the greater part of the human race had not heard of the "plan of salvation" and must be plunged into hell forever? Besides, according to the tenets of the "orthodox" church, the millions in Christian lands, who had heard of the Gospel plan, but had rejected it, were also to be in hell everlastingly. There they were to suffer untold agony, knowing that they might have been saved, and yet that they had refused the proffered mercy. And, what made it still worse was that many whom I greatly admired, in past ages and in the present, had never accepted Christ, and must therefore be damned forever. There was no hope of course for Socrates, Plato, and Confucius; for Zoroaster, Regulus, and Marcus Aurelius; for Jefferson, Hume, and Gibbon; for Shelley, John Stuart Mill, and Ralph Waldo Emerson! Of course Catherine de Medicis, Philip Second, and Judge Jeffreys were all right, for they were washed in the blood of Jesus before departing this life. How I worried over Shakespeare's doom! There seemed to be a little hope for him, because he said in his will that he "hoped through the only merits of Jesus Christ his Savior to be made partaker of life 'everlasting.'" Real character and lofty aspirations seemed to have nothing to do with our condition in the next life, according to orthodox Christianity. Those who had not gone through one little gate, of which billions of the human race had never even heard, were to be in hell, suffering inexpressible agony, and growing more wicked, forever and ever! What a horrible state of affairs! What an awful universe! And what an unreasonable God! An outlook like

this made life beyond the grave a horror rather
than a boon.

Well, the years went on and on. "The young
may die soon: the old must," came with ever increasing power to my despairing self. Weighing
what real evidence I then had, looking at the pro's
and con's, I thought it more than probable that
when the body died, we knew no more. Of course
reason testified to a spirit power working in the
universe. I thought that power animated our
bodies for a little while, and that when the body
dissolved, its portion of power returned to the universal source, and, destitute of all individuality,
knew no more. This, my friends, formed the sad
undercurrent of my thoughts, up to the autumn of
1887.

The year before, a youth of nineteen passed
away after suffering two years with consumption.
I had been intimate with his mother's family during
seven years, and had known him well from his thir-
teenth year. During his long illness, I visited him
often, and he had great confidence in my friendship
for him. Knowing that he could not get well, I
spoke many times to him of the love of Jesus, and
tried to have him accept the plan of salvation. I
wanted him to be safe, *in case* Christianity were
true. He was patient, loving, and thoughtful, but
gave not the slightest evidence of conversion. He
heard all I had to say, listened kindly through love

for me, but took no interest in what I called religious matters.   According to the tenets of Calvinism,
he had rejected the only way of salvation, tenderly
and clearly presented to him, and must go to hell.
According to the New England Primer,

"His dear soul in hell must lie,
With devils to eternity."

In the fall of 1887, his mother attended a séance
for materialization.   She declared to me that she
had seen and talked with this dear son, who passed
away in 1886.   I told her it was utterly impossible,
and I described to her the mechanical contrivances
of rubber bags, robes, wigs, and masks, by which
these frauds were accomplished.   She persisted that
she had seen George, that his clothes were like
those he wore in the coffin, that he talked like himself, and that she knew it was he.   She insisted that I
attend a séance.   I pitied her incredulity, and went
with her, in order to find out the fraud.   I believed
it to be a deception.   Still, if life beyond the grave
could be demonstrated to me, I thought I would be
very glad.   I went several times, but kept in the
background with the sceptics.   The fifth time I attended, George came from the cabinet, talked with
his mother, and asked for me.   I went up to the
cabinet, and saw that it was indeed my friend
George.   The light was good, I recognized him
perfectly, but I saw that he looked wan and very
weak.   He looked as he did the days before he

died.   He was at least four feet away from the cabinet, with his back to the cabinet, and his mother
stood facing him and was talking with him.   He
was also talking.   I stood by his side, in such a position that I saw how far he was from the cabinet.   I
was so close to him that my dress touched the lower
part of him.   It was indisputably my friend George.
He was quite tall, as in life.   He talked with his
mother.   I was looking at him, and listening to
each word.   Suddenly he became much shorter.
Then, he bowed, *and went into nothingness without
going back into the cabinet.*   I was never so astonished in my life.   "Where is he?" I exclaimed.
Bear in mind that I recognized him, that he was
palpable, that he was talking, and that he demate-
rialized *then* and *there*, and that he did *not* go back
into the cabinet, where the medium was.

My friends, this wonderful occurrence demonstrated to me that beings do exist, under different
conditions from our own; and that the so-called
dead boy was not dead, but alive; that he still loved
his mother, and that he could return.   And if this
George retained his identity after his physical body
had died, then surely my father, with his strongly
marked individuality, and my whole-souled mother,
were alive too, still loved me, and might sometimes
come near their child.

This occurrence not only demonstrated spirit existence without our kind of a body, and spirit return,

but it also overthrew the orthodox doctrines regarding salvation and hell.   Bear in mind that this George was not a Christian, that he had not accepted Christ as his Savior.   Yet here he was, free to come, declaring himself happy.   Calvinistic theology, from that moment, lost its power over me.

At the time of this demonstration, I knew nothing of Spiritualism.   I had not examined its laws. How George had been enabled to return, I had no notion.   I simply took the evidence of my senses, and trusted them on this occasion, as I have trusted them during my whole life.   That I really saw my friend, and that his body did dematerialize on the spot, as our bodies cannot do, was as certain as anything that I ever saw with my eyes on any other occasion.   To accept the evidence of my eyes on all other occasions, and to deny it on this one occasion, only because I had made up my mind beforehand that a dead person cannot materialize, would be to make myself a slave to a prejudice.

The only question to be settled here is whether the testimony of the senses of a person "of sound disposing mind and memory" is to be taken as evidence.   Supposing a person is on trial for murder, and a sane and reliable person testifies that he saw the accused drive a knife into the body of the victim, and that the victim fell down dead.   Would you take the testimony of that sane and reliable person on that question?   Has not many a man been hanged for murder on the testimony of a person who saw the murder committed? Again, if there were a person on the jury who had made up his mind beforehand that no testimony whatever could prove the guilt of the accused, would you think that person fit to sit in the jury-box on this occasion? The testimony of a sane and truthful person will be taken as evidence by all persons, except those who have deprived themselves of the power of judging fairly, by making up their minds before they have heard that evidence.

With regard to the testimony on the facts that prove spirit return, we hear church people or materialists remark, "Oh! I presume you *think* you saw this thing." A person who allows himself to so speak makes himself a slave to prejudice, and stultifies his mind. Supposing a man says to his wife, "I saw Mr. A. to-day." She replies, "Oh! I presume you *think* you saw him." Would not that man feel somewhat insulted? Supposing you attend a concert and say on your return, "I heard Miss B. sing at the musicale." Your friend replies, "Oh! I presume you *think* you heard her sing." Would you feel that you were treated fairly?

My friends, Francis Bacon in his "Novum Organum" speaks of the dens and caves in which the human mind may be shut up. Some of these dens are almost unavoidable, as they are made by the century in which a man lives, or the race to which he belongs. When these dens are brought to our notice, it behoves a man who prides himself on his reason and his clear judgment to get himself out of them just as far as possible. Let us be ready to receive the truth, if it be the truth, no matter what prejudice it may offend, and no matter what tenet of the old theology it may disprove. If the dead return, we want to know it. If they can manifest their love to us, and influence our lives for good, it is a blessed thing. And remember that no pre-conceived opinion against a fact can have any possible weight, when that fact can be proved by the same evidence that you would consider reliable if you had no prejudice against the fact.

Was that form my friend George? I knew him well, the light was good, my eyes are good, I was close to him, and I declare that it was George. Did the body of the aforesaid George, whom I recognized to be George, dematerialize at my feet, in a way that our physical bodies can not demateralize? Yes; it did so dematerialize, in the light and under the conditions aforesaid. Will my bigoted Baptist friend or my skeptical materialistic friend now say, "Oh! I presume you *think* you saw him." Well, whether another take my testimony or no, what I saw and heard convinced *me* at least that the so-called dead are not dead, that they can return, and that those who do not accept Christ as a Savior are not shut up in hell.

I had gained much, for I now knew that one at least who had died retained his separate individuality. And if George, a feeble boy, did so, surely my idolized father and my precious mother must be alive somewhere. And if George could communicate with his mother, could not my parents, though much longer in spirit life, communicate with their child? I began to hope that they could, but how this could be accomplished was the question. How could they communicate thoughts to me that would prove that it was they, and no one else, that was dealing with me?

Friends, let us first inquire how one of our minds gives its thought to another mind? My mind is shut up in my body. You cannot see my mind. How can my mind give you its thought? We can conceive of but two ways. One way is for my mind to impart its thought to yours, without any physical agency at all,—in other words, exactly as if your mind and mine were wholly freed from our bodies. I say we can conceive of that way. And by and by, when we shall be in spirit life, we shall not only conceive of that way, but we shall practice it. And as a Spiritualist, I know that my spirit friends do often give me their thoughts in this way, by pure impression, their spirit impressing my spirit.

What is the only other way by which my mind can give your mind its thoughts? Our reply is, by the use of some physical sign which may represent

that thought. Suppose I look at you and smile.
You know by that that I am pleased in my mind.
Did you see my mind? You saw the movement of
certain portions of my physical face; and those
movements, producing what we call a smile, formed
a physical sign, by which you knew that I, *whom
you cannot see*, was pleased. You ask me a question. I wish to reply in the affirmative. I bow my
head, a mere physical sign of what my mind feels.
Or I say "yes," a sound made by particular movements of my vocal organs, which set waves of air in
motion and affected your organs of hearing in a particular way; and by these physical acts, your mind
learns that my mind assents to your question. Or,
I write "yes" on paper or slate, and you see those
signs with your eyes, and you know that those
marks that you ·see with your physical eyes mean
that my mind assents to the question of your mind,
which you had asked of me by some physical means.
And, is there anything in the sound of the word
"yes," or anything in the way it looks, that makes
it mean assent, any more than the word "no" would
do? A Frenchman expresses assent by a totally
different sound, "oui;" and an Italian, by the word
"si." And "oui" and "si" do not look like assent,
when written, any more than our word "yes."
Words, then, are arbitrary signs of thoughts or
ideas. And yet it is by these arbitrary and physical

sounds and sights that our minds communicate thoughts to one another.

Supposing now that my mind is in New York and yours in London. You want me to know that you, that is, that your mind in your physical body, reached the other side of the Atlantic in safety. You send a telegram by sub-marine wires. How is this done? By intermitting the flow of the electric fluid by longer or shorter periods, another system of arbitrary physical signs, the operator gets words, puts them on paper by written words; the paper is carried to me; I read these written signs with my physical eyes, and then my mind learns that you reached London in safety.

Is it not evident that while you and I are in the physical body, our minds must communicate thought to one another by some physical means, some facial expression, some gesture, some spoken or written words? And are not these thoughts given by arbitrary signs?

Now, let us suppose that I am still in the body, and that I have a friend who is freed from the physical body, but who loves me, and wants to communicate to me that he still lives, and cares for me. How can he do it? There are two ways. He may give me impressions on my pure spirit. But I am not yet advanced enough to know that when I have a vivid thought and at the same moment a flash of remembrance of my friend, it is probably his mind impressing my mind.   Not being experienced enough in spiritual life to understand that, how can my friend communicate his thought to me? He can do it only by physical signs, and to these signs we attach arbitrary meanings.   I ask questions by telegram.   I get "yes," or "no," or "I do not know," by dots or short lines or long lines variously combined, and the operator tell me what it means.   I want my spirit friend to answer my questions, and he must of course use the physical means at his command.   A few of us in the physical body sit around a table, our bodies well, our minds in harmony.   Our magnetism flows smoothly from one to another, and permeates the table.   My spirit friend knows the laws of magnetism better than we do.   Attendant spirits combine his magnetism with ours.   The table moves or stops at the will of these spirit operators.   We ask the question desired with our physical mouth and they reply by spirit telegraphy.   Having agreed on certain arbitrary signs, we and they know that one tip or rap of the table means "no,'" that three tips or raps mean "yes," and that two tips or raps mean "I don't know." Names, words, and whole sentences can be easily communicated by the celestial operators.   One of the mortals repeats the alphabet very slowly, and the spirit band rap at the right letter.

Is this silly?   Then the ticks of the telegraphic machine are silly too.   Is this unworthy them and

us?   Then making noises with tongue and lips and
vocal chords and air, in order to communicate
thought, is silly too.

But I must hasten. The mother of George, another lady, and myself, began to set this simple telegraphic machine for operation. We sat every
Saturday evening. The week's work done, with
true hearts, with prayer to the Great Spirit for aid,
we set the door ajar for our loved ones to come.
We invited no mediums. We each knew that the
others wanted the truth. We sat, and with loving
uplifted souls awaited the results. Tiny raps came,
that we knew *we* did not make. George came, and
by gentle and clear raps gave answers to the questions of his happy mother.

One blessed evening, the fifth time we sat together, my father came. By loud, firm, strongly
individual tips of the table, our hands lightly resting
on it, and the table always tipping *from* me, so that
I might know that *I* did not do it unconsciously, my
father came. In answer to my eager questions, he
gave unmistakably and decisively, names connected
with our life in Burmah, names totally unknown to
my two companions. In one case, the name was
unknown to me, and I verified it afterwards by
searching in his Memoirs. He even gave the last
sacred words of my mother,* in reply to his ques-

---

* "She replied in the affirmative, by a peculiar expression of her own."
Pages 245 and 246 of "Memoir of Sarah B. Judson," by Emily C. Judson.

tion whether she still loved him. These words, too sacred for publication, were never given to the world, but have lived all these years in her daughter's heart.

And how inexpressibly happy was I made by this blessed hour! Yes; my father yet lives. He loves me. He cares for me still. He teaches me and guides me. And when God shall call me to leave this mortal life, my father has promised me that he and my mother will be the first to meet me and guide me in the new spirit life. No more death, but "life forevermore!" Ah! my friends, has not Spiritualism made me happy indeed?

"The music of thy daughter's voice,
    Thou'lt miss for many a year;
And the merry shout of thy elder boys,
    Thou'lt list in vain to hear.

"But who shall paint our mutual joy,
    On yon celestial plain,
When the loved and parted here below
    Meet, ne'er to part again."

MRS. SARAH B. JUDSON.

THERE IS NO DEATH.

"There is no death! The stars go down
　　To rise upon some fairer shore;
And bright in heaven's jewelled crown
　　They shine forevermore.

"There is no death! The dust we tread
　　Shall change beneath the summer showers
To golden grain or mellowed fruit,
　　Or rainbow-tinted flowers.

"The granite rocks disorganize,
　　And feed the hungry moss they bear;
The forest leaves drink daily life,
　　From out the viewless air.

"There is no death! The leaves may fall,
　　And flowers may fade and pass away;
They only wait through wintry hours,
　　The coming of the May.

"There is no death! An angel form
　　Walks o'er the earth with silent tread;
He bears our best loved things away;
　　And then we call them 'dead.'

"He leaves our hearts all desolate,
　　He plucks our fairest, sweetest flowers;
Transported into bliss they now
　　Adorn immortal bowers.

"The bird-like voice, whose joyous tones
　　Made glad these scenes of sin and strife,
Sings now an everlasting song,
　　Around the tree of life.

"Where'er He sees a smile too bright,
　　Or heart too pure for taint and vice,
He bears it to that world of light,
　　To dwell in Paradise.

"Born into that undying life.
　　They leave us but to come again;
With joy we welcome them the same,—
　　Except their sin and pain.

"And ever near us, though unseen.
　　The dear, immortal spirits tread;
For all the boundless universe
　　Is life. *There are no dead.*"
　　　　　　　—EDWARD BULWER-LYTTON.

LECTURE V.

In the course of life, we converse with many different church members on the doctrines they are taught. Do we find that they all believe exactly the creed of the denomination to which they belong? We know very well that many members of orthodox churches "in good and regular standing" find themselves totally unable to accept all of those doctrines. Some are honest enough to say that they do not really believe all that the church teaches. Some succeed in closing their minds to all the outside influences of this progressive age, and persuade themselves that they do actually believe that far the larger share of the human race are to be tormented in hell forever, because they did not happen to go through one little gate. Others believe what they can, shut their eyes to the rest, and congratulate themselves that at any rate they are safe. For fear of seeing something dangerous, they close their eyes and hope for the best.

But sometimes a church member of this latter class loses a dear one by death, who was not in the ark of safety. For instance, we have in mind a family who lost their senior member by death, a few years ago. This old man was rich, and he was often generous to those in need. He was a considerate and loving husband and brother, and a kind and just father. He was strictly honest in all his dealings, and was highly respected in the city in which he lived. His wife, his sister, his son, and all his relatives, so far as we know, were members of the Calvinistic Baptist church. But this old man was different from all the rest. He was a free-thinker, an agnostic. He did not pretend to believe any of the "saving" doctrines of the church, had no settled belief in a life after the death of the body, and died unsaved, as far as Jesus and blood-washing are concerned. He had, however, no anxiety about the future. He knew that he had been honest and kind, and on the strength of just that, and no more, he went alone into eternity. He never professed conversion. He did not want conversion.

Now, what effect did the death of this old man have on the surviving members of his family? If they really believed as they professed to believe, the husband, brother, father, and friend had refused salvation through Jesus, and had gone to hell to stay there in agony forever. Did these surviving friends show any anxiety? Did they feel any anxiety? They manifested none. If they felt any, they calmed it by the thought that it must surely be well, somehow, with their husband, father, brother, and

friend. They were tranquil, and seem to-day just
as happy as if this old man had been thoroughly
converted, baptized, and had died avowing his trust
in the blood of Jesus.   Do these relatives of the
dead man actually believe the doctrines of their
church? If asked, they would earnestly declare
that they do accept them in full.   But, do they
really believe them?

Take another case.   We know a lady high in the
Presbyterian church, who lost her only child by
death.   The lady is a Christian.   The child was a
Christian.   But, this lady suffered agonies for years
from the dread that her child did not exist at all,
after her body was laid in the grave.   No words of
the Bible, no teachings of the church, no suggestions
offered by friends gave her the assurance that she
craved, that her child still lived somewhere.   Her
grief was terrible, and nearly destroyed her health.
All her life, she had supposed that she did believe
all that her church taught.   She had given her time,
her money, her great talent, to church work.   But,
when her little child's body died, all her props were
swept away, and she cried aloud in her anguish, "If
I could only know that my little girl is alive!"   We
are glad to state that Spiritualism has given her the
assurance she craved, and that the storm is settling
into a great calm.   It is by such baptisms of suffering that the angel world is preparing mortals to accept the blessed truth, that life *is* forevermore.

Such instances, which might be multiplied by ten thousand, show us that many church members do not in their hearts actually believe the teachings of their particular church.

An original thinker has written a book on "Religion and Dogma," the title of which conveys the thought that the "pure and undefiled" religion of which the apostle James speaks, is a very different thing from a dogma. While we all know that a true religion is founded on absolute truths, we must distinguish those absolute truths from mere dogmas.

How does a dogma differ from a truth? The ordinary meaning attached to the word dogma is that of something declared to be true by some settled and indisputable authority. And the authority which has laid down religious dogmas for us is the church. The long existing and still continued controversy between reason and authority lies in the question whether a thing is true because it is reasonable, or because the church has said that it is true. The life-long controversy between those two great lights of the twelfth century, Abelard and St. Bernard, was on this point.

St. Bernard contended for the authority of the church. Under the influence of his worderful eloquence, the Second Crusade was undertaken by France and Germany. Even those who did not understand the French tongue in which he spoke, were moved by his looks, his tones, and the cross he bore.   He founded one hundred and sixty monasteries.   So faithful was he to the Church that Dante places him high in the ninth heaven of his Paradise, "robed in glory."   What the church had decreed, Bernard held to; what the church anathematized, Bernard condemned.   Sincere, fervid, devoted, he yet placed the decision of church councils higher than human reason, and thus bound faster yet the fetters of the mind.

Very different were the views of Abelard. (Poor fellow! One never sees the "Saint" prefixed to *his* name!)   Abelard did not dare, in the twelfth century, with Medieval darkness at its depth and the power of the Papal See at its height, to separate from the church.   Probably the thought of doing so never once occurred to him.   But Abelard did venture to suggest that it might be well to inquire somewhat into the reason of things.   He did venture to hint that the authority of the church was not all that should be considered.   His powerful mind laid down the principle that "nothing is to be believed but what has been first understood," while the church held that we must believe in order to understand.   Bernard, on the contrary, said inquiry should be altogether banished from the province of religion.   Of course the two were opposed to one another; and, as Bernard had the church to support his side, he had the satisfaction of seeing Abelard imprisoned for heterodoxy.

Well! Dante does not put Abelard high in heaven. He makes no allusion whatever to him. If he had put him anywhere, we fear it would have been in the sixth circle of the Inferno, along with the arch-heretics, in tombs of fire, the covers of which were to be forever closed after the day of judgment. Such horrible retribution did the Medieval church prescribe for those who presumed to set human reason above her authority. But, thanks to the infinite source of life and light, the ·Dark Ages have gone by; and in this free United States, towards the end of this pregnant nineteenth century, men, and women too, may think for themselves, and may also dare to express their thoughts to the world.

Abelard may be considered the earliest rationalist. He first dared to assert the supremacy of reason. The tiny seed he ventured to plant in the minds of thousands of disciples sprouted into a vigorous sapling in Luther, who builded so much "better than he knew;" sprang into a magnificent tree when Thomas Paine gave his "Age of Reason" to the world; and will before very long shelter all nations with its shade, and feed all people with its fruit. Bless the angel-world for Abelard! He did good work for them, in spite of certain imperfections, which were incidental to his physical nature; and he is now in a brighter, freer sphere than the limited and partial heaven pictured by Dante.

Well, a dogma is something that may or may not

be true, though it is declared to be true by some established authority. This being the case, we apprehend the meaning attached to the words dogmatism and dogmatic. To show how a dogma and a truth differ from each other, it may be said that some of the dogmas of the church are true, while some of them are not true: also, that while some truths have been embodied in the dogmas of the church, yet it is equally true that some underlying, imperishable, and everlasting truths have never yet been embodied in the dogmas of any church that has ever existed in this world. The religion of the the future may have some of these truths expressed in form. But the great religion now developing into existence will have one cardinal feature. It will not be creed-bound. It will be ever ready for new truths and for broader views of old truths. It will be forever progressive.

Now, what is the criterion by which we are to judge of any view or statement regarding spiritual life, that is brought to our notice? We know of but two ways. We may compare it with the dogmas of some church-creed or system, or with the statements made in some special book that was composed by many different men, in Asia, many hundred years ago. That is one way of judging any statement pertaining to spiritual life.

Another way is to bring this proposed view or statement under the light of human reason, to examine it by that light, and to pronounce on its truth or falsity, according as it stands in that light.

But, the ministers will exclaim, "That is not a safe thing to do. Human reason is blinded, and liable to err." Well, friends, if we cannot depend on our reason, really what have we to depend on? We depend on our reason, in deciding matters that have to do with daily life; and, if we make mistakes, it is because we follow the impulses of passion and selfishness, and shut our eyes willfully to the clear dictates of reason.

How may we know what is the right? Simply by finding out what is reasonable. Is this unsafe, unorthodox doctrine? If it be, we have some very orthodox thinkers to bear us company. We suppose that Amherst College, Mass., would not have an unsafe man for its President. Let us see what President Seelye considers the standard of ultimate right. This orthodox New England divine, President of an orthodox college, in the co-operative revision of the "System of Moral Science," written by Dr. Hickok, another orthodox divine, agrees with him in taking the following as the standard of the ultimate right: "A reasonable being ought to act reasonably." Thanks to these good men for daring, with Abelard and Thomas Paine, to go to reason itself, rather than to any book, or council, or Almighty God himself, in order to know what is right! Right are they on this point; and, when freed from the bonds and prejudices of earth, we shall see them

"Sailing with supreme dominion
Thro' the azure deeps of air,"

on other points not yet acknowledged in their philosophy.

Dr. Wayland and Confucius found the ultimate right in the proper relation of things; Jonathan Edwards, in moral beauty; Des Cartes, in the revealed will of God. Closely allied to the view of Hickok and Seelye is the "immediate beholding of the right," adopted by Kant, as well as by Coleridge, the poetic seer of our century. But better than theirs is the statement, "A reasonable being ought to act reasonably;" for, to quote the words of the reverend authors, the ultimate right thus apprehended is simple, immutable, and universal. Instead of taking for the standard of ultimate right, the authority of the government, with Hobbes; the most productive of happiness, with Bentham; or an inward awe of the Deity, with Schlegel, these men think that the reasonable is the right, and that the sublime ought of a reasonable being (whether finite or infinite, we shall add) is to act reasonably.

But, how can I tell what is reasonable? Why, by your own reason. What! am I not to go to my Bible, to know what is right? No. use your own reason. Why, cannot I go to my pastor or my priest, in order to know what is right? No: use

your own reason. What! cannot I ask God what
is right? Certainly. But how will you ask infinite
spirit? Only by looking into your own finite spirit
and seeing what it says. *Use your own reason.*

But, you fear that your own reason is not to be
depended on. Then, whose reason are you going
to depend on? On somebody else's? If you wish
to walk, and have poor legs, do you try to walk
with the legs of somebody else? No: you walk as
well as you can, with your own. And using them
will make them improve.

The reason of all of us who are yet on the earth
plane is more or less prejudiced by our country, our
age, our race, our surroundings, our own physical
condition. But with all these disadvantages, it is
our reason, it is ours to use, and it should be our
guide. Where did it come from? It came from
the fount of infinite reason, of which it is an individualized portion. It is in the deepest sense our own
birth-right. Let us then free it from its shackles,
let us develop and strengthen it by use, let us obey
its dictates, instead of the dictates of unreason and
folly, and it will lead us aright.

It is impossible to predicate the conclusions of
minds that are enthralled by prejudice. But we
know that all others will admit that religious and
spiritual statements should be tested by the reason.
So we will proceed to consider some of the dogmas
of the church. Which of them are reasonable, and

therefore may be true; and which of them are unreasonable, and therefore false? The existence of
infinite being, embracing all finite being, was treated
of in a previous lecture. To deny such an existence,
which accounts reasonably for all individual and
finite beings, would be unreason. As David said,
such a denial could be made only by a fool. With
churches that rise to such a conception of God as is
expressed by the term, "Infinite Being," we have
no quarrel. Rather does the consciousness of such
a common source bind lovingly together all the
happy souls who share it. This consciousness belongs to the most spiritual followers of all the great
religions of the world, among which we may name
Buddhism, Christianity, and Spiritualism.

But, let us consider the basic dogma which belongs exclusively to Christianity, the dogma on
which rests the authority for all the rest. We
mean, of course, the dogma that all the books of the
Old and New Testament were directly inspired by
God himself. One of the recent supporters of this
theory writes as follows: "Every verse of the Bible,
every word of it, every syllable of it, every letter of
it, is the direct utterance of the Most High." Can
this view, or even the more moderate views of the
inspiration of the Bible by God, be shown to be reasonable? If shown to be unreasonable, it is not
right, and is therefore not a true statement. Is this
dogma reasonable, or is it not so? This dogma,

that Infinite Wisdom, Light, and Life, inspired this Bible is unreasonable, from the following considerations.

The Bible directly contradicts itself, as in the two accounts of the circumstances attending the death of Judas.   According to Matthew 27: 5-10, Judas hanged himself, and the chief priests took the thirty pieces of silver that he had earned by betraying his master, and went and bought the potter's field. But in Acts 1: 18, we are told that Judas himself bought the field with the reward of his iniquity, and died by a fall which ruptured him.   Which account is true?   One account says that the priests bought the said field after the death of Judas.   The other account says that Judas bought it himself.   Can both these propositions be true?   Instead of identical, it seems to us that we have contradictory statements, and it is impossible that both be true.

Again, we are told in Matt. 10: 10, that Jesus told his disciples not to take any staves with them, when they went on their missionary journey; while we are told in Mark 6: 8, that they must take nothing *but* a staff.   Which account is correct?   Both cannot be right, as they contradict each other.   It may be said that these are unimportant circumstances.   Granted: but do we not teach our children to be truthful in all their statements, in small as well as in large?   A slight circumstance may still make all the difference between a truth and a lie.   Commentators say that errors have crept in in copying. That is undoubtedly true. How shall we know then what statements were originally inspired by God, and which have crept in in copying? They tell us we must decide what belong to the original by seeing what cohere together. Very well: how can we judge what statements do cohere, except by using our human reason?

Is the Bible inspired by God? Certain passages inculcate revengeful feeling, as the one hundred and ninth Psalm. In the tenth verse of this Psalm, David, called "the man after God's own heart," hopes that the (innocent) children of his enemy may continually be vagabonds and beg; and in verse twelve, that there may be none to favor his fatherless children. Not satisfied with such evil wishes for the children of one he hates, he bethinks himself in verse fourteen, to wish evil to the ancestors of his enemy; and, by a refinement of cruelty, he hopes that the sin of the mother of his enemy may not be blotted out. To illustrate the revengful and bloody nature of some of these ancient writings, we remember hearing of a godly Northern clergyman who said during the Civil War that the only way he could relieve his feelings was by reading over some of the imprecatory Psalms. David never seems to forget his enemies. Even in the much read Twenty-third Psalm, otherwise very beautiful, he congratulates himself in verse five, that a table is prepared before him in the presence of his enemies.

The loving Nazarene taught that a very different state of heart is right. But, according to the Old Theology, *all* the Bible is inspired by God.

We have not time to linger on this prolific subject. We all know that in some passages the Jews were commanded to take revenge by murdering enemies who had already submitted. It is unreasonable that such commands were inspired by the infinite source of love and light and life. It is also unreasonable that to one nation alone should be given the only Bible inspired by God himself. God made all men, all are the offspring of infinite life, all are the objects of infinite care. God would not give his word to one nation alone, and not to others, because that would be a partial act and not right. Ought not *infinite* reason to act reasonably?

We do not wish to be misunderstood. The Bible, in spite of its errors, its inconsistencies, its sometimes inadequate presentation of the acts and commands of infinite reason, in spite of its many inequalities, is still probably the best of all compilated works, so far. But, that it was all inspired by Infinite Wisdom is unreasonable.

The Spiritualistic view of the inspiration of the Bible is wholly reasonable. What is that view? It is that the writers of the Old and New Testaments were all what we now call mediums. In other words, they were sensitive to disembodied spirit influence. But it was not infinite spirit that inspired them. They were inspired by various spirits, who had once been human beings in the flesh. Freed from the bondage of the body, they continued to love those in earth life, especially those who belonged to their own race, or those who were allied to them in aspiration after the spiritual. These disembodied spirits were of different grades of intelligence and goodness, just as one twinkling star differs from another star in the power of radiating light. This view, that different finite spirits inspired the different parts of the Bible, accounts for the inconsistencies and the inequalities in a reasonable way. It also accounts for the loftiness of the more spiritual portions. Of course these Hebrew mediums drew inspiration from various classes of spirits, according to their own varying conditions.

For instance, David, being exceedingly impressional, while extraordinarily composite in his own nature, writes very differently at different times. He did indeed play upon a harp of a thousand strings, though he was always emotional. When inclined to tender devotion, he drew a kindred class of spirits, and expressed pure devotion. But when he was aroused by the unjust opposition of his foes, he became the medium of hateful, vengeful spirits, and wrote the "imprecatory Psalms" alluded to above. Personally endowed with imagination and a love of

Nature, he voiced to mortals the sublime conception of a Deity manifest in all his works, as in the 19th and the 104th Psalm.

"Like attracts like," is one of the laws of the spiritual world, and an inspirational medium who wishes to elevate the race should keep his heart so loving and his aspirations so pure that only the best inspiration can be expressed through his mediumship. Jesus was an almost ideal sensitive, and nearly all that is recorded as coming from his lips is fitted to elevate and bless mankind.

We cannot dwell longer on this, the true view of the inspiration of the Scriptures, but we are sure that it will commend itself to the thinking, the unprejudiced, and the fearless mind.

We must hasten to show the unreasonableness of a few other dogmas of the church, and also show how the Spiritualistic view of the subject is the reasonable view, and therefore likely to be the true one. We will first consider the fall of man.

> " In Adam's fall,
> We sinned all."

This doctrine means that at first man was made sinless and perfect. He knew nothing whatever of evil, being forbidden to taste even of the tree of the knowledge of good and evil. An ideal man, he was placed in a beautiful garden, with an ideal woman. They were then allowed to fall, and became totally depraved, involving all their posterity to the end of time in their own depravity, said cognate and innate depravity making them the fit subjects of eternal woe. This doctrine is unreasonable, because "a reasonable being ought to act reasonably." We are taught by it that an infinitely reasonable and powerful being made a mistake in his method of creation. He meant to make "very good," and alas! it came out very bad. Having made a mistake, he then had to contrive some way of undoing his own work, for a small portion at any rate, of the billions of created human beings. This method is called by some "the plan of salvation."

The doctrine of the fall of man is also unreasonable by analogy. Everything else in creation, from nebulæ to worms, begins low down in the scale, and is gradually developed. But, according to this doctrine, man was, against all analogy, created perfect at once, and then descended from ideal perfection to a very low condition, with a heavy stone chained to his neck, that would hold him forever in the depths of perdition, unless a separate miracle be wrought for each individual. My friends, if we engaged some one to construct a thing for us, and he made such wretched work as this, we should not employ him the second time.

What is the Spiritualistic view of this same subject? It is that the life of every human being is an individualized drop from the ocean of infinite life. It is in its origin but a germ. But, that germ has

infinite possibilities in it. Circumstances may delay
the development of that germ. But, sharing in infinite life, it can never die, it can never be "lost."
Sometime, somewhere, it will have opportunity for
development. The germ is "very good," and its
full maturity will be still better. This development
view is in accordance with the general laws of nature, it is eminently reasonable, and is therefore far
more likely to come from Infinite Reason than the
old and pernicious dogma of the fall of man.

Is the doctrine of the Deity of Jesus reasonable?
Is it reasonable that the finite be infinite, and that
the infinite be finite? We are told that it is a mystery and beyond our comprehension. Of course the
infinite is beyond our comprehension. But we can
at least see that it is not finite. If Almighty God
should tell us that two and two made five, should
we be bound to accept that statement because it is
called a mystery? There are things that are mys-
terious to us, hemmed in as we are by flesh limitations; but do not let us make a mystery out of an
absurdity. The Spiritualistic view of Jesus is natural, reasonable, and true. He was the most perfect medium between mortal man and the spirit
world that we know of. Pure, candid, and unselfish,
he was filled with the spirit of good to his full,
though finite capacity, and was indeed a manifestation of the God Spirit in a human being. He
claimed that, when he said, "I and my father are

one." And he claimed no more than that, for he
said, "My father is greater than I," and also, "I in
them (his disciples), and thou in me, that we all
may be made perfect in one."

Is the atonement a reasonable doctrine? Is it
just that persons who do wrong can get out of the
consequences by appropriating to themselves the
good deeds that some other being does? Kant felt
that this substitutionary virtue was immoral, and we
quite agree with him. It also causes immorality.
It is pernicious to morals to let persons get the notion that their future condition depends on something besides their own conduct. It is wicked to
teach such false notions to children. It is such
teachings as these that excuse the newspapers of the
United States for presuming that a bank defaulter
must, during some part of his career, have been a
Sunday-school superintendent. What! commit a
wrong act, and then expect the legitimate consequence of that act to be washed away by the blood
of Jesus!

Spiritualism shows us that our future condition
will depend on our own conduct while here. Spiritualism teaches the *reign of law*, and not the anarchy
of injustice. We also know that ample opportunities
will be presented to all spirits, by those more advanced, to atone for their wrong, and cruel, and unjust acts. Progression is the law of the spirit world.
The germ of good is implanted in every soul, and

each soul will have an eternity for its development.
The rapidity of that development will depend on the
efforts and the earnestness of each soul. Each
spirit will gradually become aware of the laws on
which spiritual progression depends, and each will
in its own good time adapt its conduct to those laws,
and enter on the eternal and upward path designed
by its Creator.

Is not this knowledge of progression more reasonable, and therefore more worthy of God, than
the old doctrine of only two fixed states of the dead?

"Shall not the Judge of all the earth do right."
Can we, *dare* we believe that a soul will be eternally
tortured, because it had no chance to develop aright
here? Bigots may assert it, but as Whittier says,

> " Nothing can be good in Him,
> Which would be evil in me."

God is good. God made us right. He made *all*,
that they may progress. What is the religion destined to be the religion of the human race? My
friends, the name of that religion is "Progressive
Spiritualism."

THE PROBLEM.

"I like a church; I like a cowl;
I love a prophet of the soul;
And on my heart monastic aisles
Fall like sweet strains, or pensive smiles;
Yet not for all his faith can see
Would I that cowled churchman be.

"Why should the vest on him allure,
Which I would not on me endure?

"Not from a vain or shallow thought
His awful Jove young Phidias brought;
Never from lips of cunning fell
The thrilling Delphic oracle;
Out from the heart of nature rolled
The burdens of the Bible old;
The litanies of nations came,
Like the volcano's tongue of flame,
Up from the burning core below,—
The canticles of love and woe;
The hand that rounded Peter's dome,
And groined the aisles of Christian Rome,
Wrought in a sad sincerity;
Himself from God he could not free;
He builded better than he knew;—
The conscious stone to beauty grew.

"Know'st thou what wove yon wood-bird's nest
Of leaves, and feathers from her breast?
Or how the fish outbuilt her shell,
Painting with morn each annual cell?
Or how the sacred pine-tree adds
To her old leaves new myriads?
Such and so grew these holy piles,
While love and terror laid the tiles.

"These temples grew as grows the grass;
Art might obey, but not surpass.
The passive master lent his hand

To the vast soul that o'er him planned;
And the same power that reared the shrine
Bestrode the tribes that knelt within.
Ever the fiery Pentecost
Girds with one flame the countless host,
Trances the heart through chanting choirs,
And through the priest the mind inspires.
The word unto the prophet spoken
Was writ on tables yet unbroken;
The word by seers or sibyls told,
In groves of oak, or fanes of gold,
Still floats upon the morning wind,
Still whispers to the willing mind.
One accent of the Holy Ghost
The heedless world hath never lost.
I know what say the fathers wise,—
The Book itself before me lies,
Old Chrysostom, best Augustine,
And he who blent both in his line,
The younger Golden Lips or mines,
Taylor, the Shakespeare of divines.
His words are music to my ear,
I see his cowled portrait dear;
And yet, for all his faith could see,
I would not the good bishop be."

—RALPH WALDO EMERSON.

LECTURE VI.

In the preceding lecture, it was shown that reason is to be applied to all statements of a moral, religious, or spiritual nature. We are always to judge them by the standard of reasonableness. If a statement be reasonable, we are free to accept it, on sufficient grounds; if not reasonable, we should not accept it on any grounds whatever.

This test is to be applied, of course, to whatever was taught by him who was, as far as we know, the best and the most spiritual of men. But the application of this test is not our present subject. On this occasion, we do not inquire whether the teachings of Jesus were in accordance with reason, and therefore likely to be true. Our simple enquiry now is, "What did Jesus really teach?"

We make this enquiry, because the church in general has presented Jesus of Nazareth as laying great stress on certain doctrines that were not really taught by him at all. The doctrines alluded to were proclaimed by certain of his followers who were led by Jewish prejudice to misconstrue his teachings. What did Jesus teach? Did he teach what the church has mainly taught these many hundred years, or did he specially teach the very things that the church has either wholly ignored, or else has made quite subordinate to what it calls the "saving" doctrines?

To understand more clearly how it came about that the church has so misconstrued his teachings, we will consider the religious views of his nation up to his time. Later, we will see what he really taught; and afterwards, how the teachings of the church since his time differ from his own.

Well then, to begin with, what were the religious views of the Jews? Jesus was himself a Jew, that is, in parentage, in education, and perhaps in all his surroundings. What were the religious views of the Jewish nation? The Jews had been in existence as a separate nation for about two thousand years. Their founder, Abraham, was a Chaldee, and therefore of the old Semitic race. Raising the veil that hides the remote past, we find there were three primitive communities: the Aryan, the Semitic, and the Turanian. The migrating Aryans settled Europe, Persia, and Hindostan. The Semites occupied the valley of the Tigris and Euphrates and the adjacent regions. The Chaldees were a mixed race, having both Semitic and Turanian blood, with a preponderance of the former. Abraham being a Chaldee, the Jews are mostly Semitic. We, being descended from the Aryans, are of a separate race from the Jews, dating back to the remotest antiquity. It seems strange indeed that while most Christian nations hold to the personal god of the Aryans, they should cling so closely to the sacred writings of a Semitic people.

The Semitic race believed originally in one God. They adored one Supreme Being, and also did homage to intermediary deities, whose function was to go between the Supreme Being and man. The Arabians being also Semitic, we are not surprised at the success of Mohammedanism among them. According to the Hebrew Scriptures, the Assyrians worshiped one Supreme God; for we read in Jonah that he preached to the people of Ninevah that God was displeased by their wickedness, and that the whole city was afraid and repented in dust and ashes. Had they been idolaters alone, Jonah would have been obliged to convert them first to a belief in God. He appealed to their fear of the God whom their wicked deeds had displeased. While our ancestors, the Aryans, believed in a personal and therefore a limited God, the Semites believed in a Supreme Being. Abraham, then, got the notion of one God from his ancestors. Being highly mediumistic, he was told by a spirit to go west, and his strongly individualized and egotistic nature led him to believe that these spiritual manifestations came from the Supreme God of his race. His migration with his family is the opening act in the drama of the Jewish race.

The posterity of Abraham went through many vicissitudes. A train of manifestations made through Jewish mediums by the spirit world led them into Egypt, and after a residence there of four hundred years, brought them to Canaan, the country to which Abraham had migrated long before.

The four hundred years in Egypt had their effect on the religious notions of this remarkable race. The original pure religion of Egypt had degenerated to the worship of many deities. The chief deity was Osiris, the representative of the ancient phallic worship, and he was worshipped mostly in the form of a bull. So the Jews became familiarized with the notion of worshiping a being in that form. We are not surprised then to find that when they lapsed into idolatry they were prone to make an idol of that form, as when Aaron made them a calf of gold at the time they thought that Moses had been destroyed by the eruption of Mt. Sinai. Jereboam, too, pandered to the notions gathered during their residence in Egypt, when he set up the calves in Dan and Bethel.

Moses, that remarkable medium of communications from the spirit world, and the first great writer of the Jewish race, was familiar with the learning of Egypt. This great man recorded his own visions of the creation, wrote up the historical traditions of his people, led the Jews from bondage, gave them their system of theology, religious ritual, and jurisprudence, led them to the borders of Canaan, and then passed, like Mohammed, to "join his companions on high," in the world of disembodied spirits.

The political existence of the Jews began with their migration from Egypt. Having seized Canaan and exterminated its patriotic inhabitants, they were ruled by judges for four hundred years, and by kings for some six hundred more. Then they were captured and carried back to the old Semitic home. The remnant that returned to Canaan were harassed by surrounding nations for perhaps four hundred years, and were at last subjugated by Rome. Few nations, perhaps no other nation, ever survived such vicissitudes.

The religion of this noteworthy race consisted of two main points. These were the existence of one Supreme Being, and that this Supreme Being was to be propitiated by sacrifices. These sacrifices were mostly of animals; and, in extreme cases, of human beings, as in the case of the nearly consummated sacrifice of Isaac, by his priest-father Abraham. There were then two fundamental ideas in the Jewish religion: one God, and the propitiation of the same by blood offerings. Before the time of Moses, they offered as many animals as they chose. Moses fixed the kind of animals and their number. An enormous number were killed every year. This daily slaughter produced such an amount of dangerous garbage, over and above the portions that were eaten by the priests, that a fire was kept burning in the valley south of the temple, to consume the refuse. This fire was burning night and day in the spot called Gehenna, and it was to this familiar fact that Jesus alluded, when he spoke of evil things being burnt up in the place where "the fire is not quenched." Every day in every year, then, the Hebrew was familiar with the notion of blood being shed, in order to propitiate offended Deity. It was a fundamental notion of his religion.

Did Jesus accept all this? Did Jesus think God was to be propitiated by a blood offering? He taught exactly contrary to this. He said it was useless to carry a gift to the altar while the giver did not love his neighbor. When he was brought at the age of twelve to see the offerings at the temple, he asked questions of the learned Jews that they were unable to answer. Later, it was in the temple that he displayed a passionate anger that seemed foreign to his nature. Its ritual displeased him, for he thought that a man's conduct in daily life was a better sacrifice than that made by slaughtering an animal. He drove the money changers out of the temple, and said that it ought to be a house of prayer for all nations, thus recognizing the universal brotherhood of man, instead of the narrow Jewish exclusiveness. See Mark 11: 17. So opposed was he to what the typical Jew considered most important, that he awoke their bitterest anger.

Theologians claim that Jesus came to this world in order to die for mankind, and to save them by his shed blood. Did Jesus come for this purpose? If he did come on purpose to do this, he must have *known* it. And yet, during the three years that he went about, teaching his disciples and the people, did he once teach them that he had come in order to shed his blood for the sins of mankind? My "orthodox" friend, you think that he thus taught. But, examine his words as recorded in the four Gospels, and not the epistles of certain Jews, penned after his execution, and see if that be the gist of his teachings. So far from declaring that he came in order to shed his blood, he declares plainly in Luke 4: 18, what he did come for. We there read, "To preach the gospel to the poor, to heal the broken-hearted, to preach deliverance to the captives, and recovering of sight to the blind, to set at liberty them that are bruised." The only word in the foregoing that can be construed to mean what the church has claimed, is the word gospel. And the meaning of that word gospel has been misconstrued persistently by the "orthodox" clergy. They insist that gospel means the "good news" that sinners can be saved from being damned forever by being washed in the blood of Jesus. The "good news" spoken of is nothing of the kind. The good news spoken of is that there was peace and good will towards men. Instead of teaching an offended Deity to be propitiated by blood, Jesus taught God's good will to us, and that we should love one another.

The forerunner of Jesus, John the Baptizer, taught repentance—another word sadly misconstrued by the "orthodox" clergy. The Greek word, metanoia, translated "repentance" in Protestant Bibles, and "do penance" in the Douay version, means, according to Greek scholars, not sorrow for sin, but a change of one's mind or governing purpose. To repent, then, is to change one's purpose in the conduct of one's life. Jesus also told them to repent, meaning to change their life.

Matthew gives us the longest report of any one of the discourses of Christ to the people. We call it the "Sermon on the Mount," and it is found in the fifth, sixth, and seventh chapters of Matthew So clearly did this discourse embody the leading opinions of Jesus on the conduct of life, that he repeated it on a plain in Galilee, as recorded in the sixth chapter of Luke. What did Jesus teach in this memorable discourse? He taught that the blessed or happy ones were the poor in spirit, the meek, the merciful, the peace-makers, the pure in heart, and those that long or hunger to be good. He taught that it was wrong to feel anger, to hate, to lie, to think lustful thoughts, and to resist evil. He taught that men ought to love their enemies, that they should do charitable deeds unknown to others, and should pray in secret. He does not say one word of shedding his blood, and of saving them in that way. He commanded men to be perfect, just like the father in heaven. He thus left them to infer that such perfection was possible, and he makes no suggestion that his own goodness was to be applied in order to make up for their moral deficiencies. He says distinctly that men are to be known by their own fruits. He does not say that they can be justified by having the righteousness of some other being imputed to them. And what he said, he said with the authority of one who knew.

When persons who had heard of his healing power came to him to be cured of their bodily diseases, he required from them or from some one connected with them the belief that he had the power to effect their cure. "Believest thou that I am able to do this?" "According to your faith be it done unto you," were among his words to those who sought his aid. Their belief that he could cure them was an essential element. Their faith made him able to do it. Conversely, when faith on their part was wanting, he could not cure. In one place, he did not many mighty works because of their unbelief. His benevolence would certainly have led him to remove all suffering, if the proper conditions could have been supplied. This remarkable medium between the material and the spiritual word could draw healing power from above in proportion to the faith exercised by those who wanted help. There were two conditions then to the success of the effort: power poured into him from above, and belief on the part of the mortal. Evidently, his own power was not enough. In fact, he had no power of his own. It was imparted to him from above, when the faith was supplied from below. Those who examine the healing effected by mediums in our own day are aware that it is now the same as in the time of the great healer of Nazareth.

Jesus was firm and courageous, and tried to inspire his followers with the same spirit. He said they must give the world what he taught them, unmindful of consequences. He said they must do good on the Sabbath day, even though work were involved in the act. He taught his followers to distinguish between the good and the bad, and said that the bad would all be eliminated in time, and be burned up.

Many have thought that his statement that the bad in us shall be burned up meant an everlasting torment by fire. Such an inference could be made only in a barbarous and cruel age. What is the use of fire as an element in nature? Is its object to give torment? Is not fire rather the great purifier? Its power is exerted in nature, not with the object of giving pain, but with the intent to transmute what is hurtful into new and beneficent forms. Fire burns up the dross, and leaves the pure metal. Fire does good. The pain that comes from a violation of law, in either the natural or the spiritual world, is reformatory, and not punitive—theologians of the old school to the contrary! Jesus said the tares in our nature will be burned up, while the wheat in us will be saved, and we are glad that it is to be so.

Jesus was a radical, and went against the teachings of the Jewish religionists of his time. He was aware that they were becoming more and more angry with him; and he, like Savonarola, foresaw his own judicial murder. If he had lived now, the church religionists of our day would scorn and hate him. They would despise a man who told the rich to give away all his money to the poor. Many of them would misconstrue the motives of a physician who could cure hundreds of dreadful diseases, and never charged a dollar for it. The church of to-day values material good, and pays the highest salary to the clergyman who can draw the best paying audience. Jesus taught that we should not desecrate spiritual things by bringing in the question of making money.

His comprehensive mind summed up the ten commandments of Moses by two directions given to the heart of man: Love God, and Love your neighbor as yourself. By the parable of the Last Judgment, a parable wrongfully taken to be a prophecy regarding a future event in the history of the world, he shows the result of showing love or hate to our neighbors. He pictures men as standing before

him as before a judge, in order to show the effect
of their conduct to other persons. According to
Calvinistic theology, those who had been washed in
the blood of Jesus would be put on the right hand,
and those who had refused to be saved in that way,
on his left hand. Does he classify men according to
any such narrow and arbitrary standard? By no
means. Those who fed and clothed, and visited
when ill and in prison, those who did as Jesus did,
would be rewarded by happiness. Those who had
neglected to do these benevolent and loving acts
were to suffer for ages and ages.

Whether Jesus intended to teach that persons
would suffer eternally is doubtful. He certainly
said that those who did not express a loving spirit
by their actions would suffer a very long time. We
are uncertain whether he thought the suffering
would be eternal, because the Greek language, by
which he expressed his thoughts, has no word or
words equivalent to our expressions, "eternal" and
"everlasting." He said in Greek that they would be
in pain for eons on eons. Our word "forever," and
the German "ewigkeit," convey an idea that cannot
be conveyed by any Greek or Latin words. An
eon is certainly a limited time, for the word can be
made plural; and no multiple of a limited period can
be synonymous with eternity. Jesus evidently
thought the pain would be very long. But the pain
was the consequence of an unloving spirit, and not

the consequence of refusing salvation through him.

Jesus did not seek an earthly kingdom. If he ever had desires of that kind they left him when he withstood the temptation to misuse his mediumship. This temptation was presented to him by a low spirit when he was in a condition of unusual susceptibility by a long fast in solitude. Once conquered, it did not recur.

He came to teach that God is spirit, and is to be adored by our spirit, and not by ritual forms. He taught that the spirit is more important than the body, because it survives the death of the body. He taught that our condition after leaving the body will depend on our own acts. He did not grasp the germ idea and the development of that germ by an infinite progression, as is done by seers of our own day. These later seers are abreast with the thought of the day, and are also taught by spirits who have profited by the precepts of Jesus during nearly two thousand years.

Jesus said that when he should be lifted up he would draw all men to himself. His followers thought that by the lifting up he alluded to his death on the cross. What he really meant by being lifted up was his being taken out of the material world. Lifted up into the spirit world, he does draw aspirational souls, and will continue to do so. His pure, self-sacrificing life, his uncomplaining death of agony, will draw hearts to him. He draws us, not because he was that dream of theologians, an incarnation of infinite God; but because he was a man, and showed what a man could be.

Well, what took place after the death of Jesus? He appeared to his disciples a few times by materialization or etherealization, told them to teach to the world what he had taught them, and directed them to stay in Jerusalem until they should receive the same powers of healing and doing other wonders that he had possessed. They followed his directions, and on the day of Pentecost, when all sitting quietly together, the power was manifested by a strong breeze and a light sitting on the head of each. Endued with the promised power, they began to preach. The burden of their preaching was to repent, or change the course of life, and by baptism avow acceptance of the teachings of Jesus, who had died, and then arisen from the dead. The mediumistic powers conferred on these disciples caused many to accept their teachings, just as the same powers are now causing many to accept the teachings of Spiritualism, which is in truth the "second coming" of the "Christ" *spirit*.

But these early disciples were Jews, and imbued with the notion of propitiating the Deity by the shedding of blood. Besides, a natural and patriotic pride made them desire that the new doctrines should be in some way combined with the ancient and glorious ritual of the Temple service. Jesus had not restored the old political freedom for which they had longed. He had died a cruel and bloody death. Might it not be that his shed blood was to be taken as the great sacrifice to propitiate angered Deity, of which the slaughter of millions of animals was the type? This thought happily reconciled such incongruous elements as the failure to establish the kingdom, the humiliating and bloody death of their leader, and the old Jewish ritual.

Then came the conversion of the apostle Paul, the man who had the strongest mind and the deepest learning of all the early disciples. Converted by a spiritual manifestation, he was forced to accept Christ. Educated at the feet of most learned Rabbis and steeped in Jewish lore, familiar with the Mosaic ritual and therefore with the notion of expiating sin by the shedding of blood, endowed with rare power of reason and generalization, he formed the system known as the Pauline theology. Its corner-stone of proof rested on the fact that Jesus, who had died, had manifested himself as alive. In his system. Paul combined with a belief in Jesus, the old Jewish notion that blood must be shed for sin. In his letters, especially the one addressed to the Hebrews themselves, he claims that all the millions of animals slain were typical of Jesus slain, and that the blood sacrifices culminated in the death of Jesus.

At the same time, the thought crept into the minds of the disciples that the man Jesus was really an incarnated Deity. That a god sometimes takes human form was a notion found in many religions. When the disciples walked with Jesus and heard him talk, they revered him, but they did not think of him as God. John, who saw his greatest "miracles," who lay on his breast in intimate friendship, and loved him with reverent devotion, did not *then* think of him as *God.* In later years, as the remembrances of his remote youth invested his wonderful friend with a divine halo, the thought grew in John that he was indeed God incarnate. Christians reasoned that the death of a mere man was not enough. Jesus had hung on the cross, shedding his blood. He had called himself son of man and son of God. It was earnestly claimed that he must have been God in-carnate, and therefore worthy of being the realiza-tion of all the previous sacrifices.

In which of the four gospels is the doctrine of the divinity of Jesus most positively maintained? If a clergyman be asked to prove from the Bible the deity of the Nazarene, to which book does he turn? He shows us passages in the gospel of John. Was John's gospel written at the time the other gospels were written? Friends, it was written long after. Matthew and Mark, who wrote their records soon after the execution of their master, give his life in detail. Luke wrote considerably later. The notion of the sacrificial character of his death had become more clearly defined; and we find that Luke brings

that element into much greater prominence than
Matthew and Mark had done.   Long after the third
Gospel had been penned, in fact about sixty years
after the crucifixion, John, in his old age, wrote the
Gospel that clearly stated the doctrine that the Nazarene was Almighty God.   That John does teach
it clearly is evident to those who give a fair inter-
pretation to his simple words.   A Unitarian who
wishes to believe that all the Bible is inspired finds
it somewhat difficult to reconcile John's words with
a merely human Jesus.   In John's extreme old age,
the thought that the wonderful man of Judea was
Deity himself had taken firm root in the church, and
he embodies it firmly in the fourth and last record
of what Jesus did and taught.

One other letter addressed to the church in general was written by James, son of Joseph and Mary,
and therefore own brother of Jesus of Nazareth.
He is called James the Just, and was martyred by
stoning about thirty years after his brother Jesus
was crucified.   His epistle differs widely from those
written by Paul, and to my mind he clings more
closely to "what Jesus really taught" than Paul did.
He advocates works, and says that true faith is to be
manifested by our acts.   He shows much of the
clear, incisive, radical spirit of his brother Jesus.
Instead of thinking that pure religion consists in believing that some one else's good works can be laid
to our credit, he says that it consists in "visiting the

fatherless and widows in their affliction, and in keeping one's self unspotted from the world." He
sternly rebukes those who hope that their naked and
hungry brothers may be clothed and fed, but who
do not give them clothing and bread. He indig-
nantly reproves those who give better seats to finely dressed persons than to the poor. He rebukes
hypocrisy and a censorious spirit and the love of
money just as Jesus had done. Like Jesus, he says
a man cannot serve God and mammon too. In fact,
we think the true teachings of Jesus have never
been summed up better than they were by this
James. It is very likely that the other disciples
thought him somewhat unsound. Instead of making the "blood of Jesus" the most important thing,
he never alludes to it at all. Like his single-eyed
brother, who was crucified for his radical teachings,
he goes to the root of the matter and says we must
be good ourselves, and that nothing else will avail.

We have no doubt Paul thought he was doing
right when he constructed that gigantic and pernicious system known as the Pauline theology. A
Jew, his national prejudices made him wish to combine the old sacrificial rites of the glorious old Temple with the clearer, purer doctrines taught by Jesus.
What the Nazarene really taught was spiritual, pure,
and true. In combining with these pure teachings
the horrible, propitiatory notions, he created a monstrosity. The wrong and false graft on the pure

plant of the doctrines of Jesus gave a wrong and
false direction to the growth of the church.   Paul
meant well, but his perversion of the Christ teachings has prevented them from doing their proper
work, for nearly two thousand years.   But, thanks
to the efforts of the spirit-world, a new light has
dawned on this generation and the old wicked prejudices are fast dropping away.   The world is beginning at last to realize the truth of that corner-
stone of "what Jesus really taught," "God is our
father: all men are brothers."

"Who fathoms the eternal thought?
    Who talks of scheme and plan?
The Lord is God! He needeth not
    The poor device of man.

"And so beside the Silent Sea
    I wait the muffled oar;
No harm from him can come to me
    On ocean or on shore.

"I know not where God's islands lift
    Their fronded palms in air;
I only know I *cannot* drift
    Beyond His love and care."

ABOU BEN ADHEM.

"Abou Ben Adhem—may his tribe increase!
Awoke one night from a deep dream of peace,
And saw, within the moonlight in his room,
Making it rich, and like a lily in bloom,
An angel writing in a book of gold.

"Exceeding peace had made Ben Adhem bold,
And to the presence in the room he said,
'What writest thou?' The vision raised its head,
And, with a look made of all sweet accord,
Answered, 'The names of those who love the Lord.'
'And is mine one?' said Abou. 'Nay, not so,'
Replied the angel. Abou spoke more low,
But cheerily still; and said, 'I pray thee, then,
Write me as one that loves his fellow-men.'
The angel wrote and vanished.

                    The next night
It came again, with a great wakening light,
And showed the names whom love of God had blessed,
And lo! Ben Adhem's name led all the rest."

—LEIGH HUNT.

LECTURE VII.

THE SPIRITUALISM OF JESUS.

Before speaking directly of the Spiritualism of the Nazarene, it seems necessary to clear away a notion that long clouded our own mind, when thinking of the acts of this remarkable being. This same notion permeates the Christian church, and deprives its members of a true view of his personality. We refer to the opinion that Jesus was in any sense supernatural. We would not wish to be wanting in reverence. We do with all our heart reverence the Nazarene. We only wish to point out clearly that he was not supernatural.

By the word supernatural is meant the quality of being beyond or outside of the forces of nature. A book by a clear-seeing thinker of our day, Henry Drummond, entitled "Natural Law in the Spiritual World," bears on this point, that all that happens, in the physical and also in the spiritual world, is under Nature's laws, and is therefore natural. The consideration that draws many minds irresistibly to Spiritualism is the reasonable and beautiful doctrine that all things, both in the body and out of the body, are subject to Nature's laws. Ought we to like what is natural? Ought we to like what is normal? A mother who is cruel to her own offspring awakens the disgust of all. We express our repugnance to her conduct by calling her unnatural. A cancer, a tumor, a diphtheritic membrane is an abnormal or an unnatural growth that finally implicates the whole system. A two-headed calf is a monstrosity. It is against the laws of nature, and cannot be seen with pleasure by a person of pure taste. We are repelled by it, while what is in accordance with law and order is pleasing to a well-balanced mind.

A common superstition is that when we leave the body we at once become outside of and beyond the laws of Mother Nature. Nothing can be further from the truth. We Spiritualists have learned that when we leave the body, we feel just as natural as we do now. Mrs. Oliphant's beautiful sketch, "A Little Pilgrim," brings out this fact in clear relief. When we experience the change called death, shall we feel as if we were dead? Not at all. Many who drop the worn body are astonished to find that they feel alive, and just the same, except that they are freer and relieved from much that annoyed them before. Feeling as alive as ever, and conscious of a body, they are quite amazed that their friends yet in the flesh do not hear their voices, and do not feel their caresses any more.

We once heard Joseph Cook say, "Nature is an

effect, of which God is the cause." Before Mr. Cook, Cowper said in "The Task,"

" Nature is but a name for an effect,
Whose cause is God."

We Spiritualists do not claim that we can comprehend God, as some of the old theologians seem to have claimed. We do not claim that we can measure absolute being, that we can analyze illimitability, and give attributes to the infinite life that pervades each and all. But we do claim that infinite life *is*, and that infinite life in motion is manifested by what we call the laws of Nature. We also claim that these natural laws pervade all beings and all worlds; all physical and all spiritual beings, as well as all physical and all spiritual worlds.

Do Spiritualists then believe in miracles? Certainly not. The devout church-member cries, "What! do you not think that Jesus did miracles?" No: we know that Jesus did no miracles. We know that Jesus did all that he did under natural laws. He violated no law, he contradicted no law. Many things that he did seemed miraculous to men who did not understand the natural laws of physical and spiritual existence so well as he did. He undoubtedly knew how to adapt himself to those laws better than most men who have walked the earth.

What is a miracle? The dictionary defines a miracle as an event or effect contrary to the constitution and course of nature. In short, it violates nature, because it is superior to it, and we call it a supernatural thing. Hume did not believe in miracles. But Hume was no atheist. He believed in God, and that God manifested himself in the laws of nature. Believing that natural law is God in action, he did not believe that the Bible could be proved to be from God, by miracles or deviations from that law. Hume believed that the laws of Nature were the true and everlasting manifestation of the Deity. He said it was therefore absurd to the last degree that God should manifest his agency in the Bible by deviating from his own laws. The church of his day said Chistianity and the Bible rested directly on these deviations from natural law. So Hume rejected the Bible, and was condemned by the clergy. But he was a truthful, humane, pure man, and was not condemned when he passed into spirit life. He was ostracized as an infidel here. But he was welcomed to pure and joyous circles when he entered the spirit-world, for his vision of universal law was clear; and while he had his experience in earth life, he endeavored to adapt his own conduct to that law.

With regard to those things related in the Bible that seem strange, we Spiritualists claim that they may be true, if they can be shown to be in accordance with the laws of nature. A better understanding of those laws, and especially of those that govern the spiritual world and its relations to this, will give a natural explanation of many things that men have thought miraculous or supernatural.

How many learned men have puzzled themselves as to what Socrates meant by his attendant spirit! It is well known that this famous Greek said he had a spirit that directed him in his conduct. He called this attendant his "daimon," a word meaning "spirit," in the Greek. Philosophers have asked what Socrates could possibly have meant by such a claim. Some of them think he meant his conscience. Others say he meant the still, small voice of God in his soul. Some think that as Socrates thought he had an attendant spirit, he was, though sane on all other points, out of his head on this one point. We are forcibly reminded here that some men in our own day and generation are considered of "sound disposing mind" on all points *except* that they are Spiritualists. Well, we will not be discouraged, brothers and sisters in Spiritualism. The tables will turn by and by. The time will come when those who are *not* Spiritualists will be the ones that the world will call unsound.

But, to return to Socrates, his attendant spirit, his "daimon," which has been such a puzzle to students of classic lore, is no puzzle to us Spiritualists. Being a good man, and a spiritual man, and also mediumistic, Socrates drew to himself a spirit of a high order, that could manifest his individual existence to him. Being clairaudiant, he could hear the voice

of this spirit directing him on important occasions.
The great mystery is no mystery at all to those who
have studied the natural laws that govern spirit manifestations. The absolute knowledge that Socrates
possessed of the immortality of the soul proves
that he had something more than reason alone to
give him that assurance. Read the "Krito" and the
"Phædo," and you will see that this noblest of the
Greek philosophers was a Spiritualist. "How do
you wish us to bury you?" asked Crito. "Just as
you please," answered Socrates, quietly laughing
and glancing at us, "if you only get hold of me, and
do not let me escape you." Socrates knew *hc*
would live after his body died, because he had seen
spirits, and knew somewhat of their mode of life.

The mystery of the "voices" and the "communications," and the "revelations" to Joan of Arc, completely disappears under the light of Spiritualism.
According to "natural law in the spiritual world,"
she was clairvoyant and clairaudiant. Being exceedingly pure, simple, and patriotic, as well as
mediumistic, spirits of the same kind were drawn to
her. Through her instrumentality, these disembodied spirits of France did deeds for their loved
country that will cause the name of the holy Maid
to be revered by patriotic Frenchmen to the end of
time.

An unprejudiced study of spirit power and spirit
manifestations will show that many things that Jesus

did may also be done by those who yield themselves
to spirit influence, and obey the laws of the spirit
world, *just as he did.*   We learn in the same way
that if Jesus is said to have done anything contrary to the laws of nature, that thing is not true.
But, before rejecting the truth of anything claimed
to have been done by him, we must be very careful
that we know the natural laws bearing on that point.
Further investigation may show men like Hume that
some of the things rejected as miraculous may really
be in accordance with natural forces not yet fully
understood.   In like manner, let us be very careful,
before rejecting any of the phenomena claimed by
Spiritualists, that we understand the natural laws
bearing on these special phenomena.   If we do reject phenomena that really rest on natural law, we
may, in Bible language, find ourselves among those
who "fight against God," for we admit that "Nature
is an effect, of which God is the cause."

In what did the Spiritualism of Jesus consist?   In
other words, what were the physical, mental, and
spiritual qualities of Jesus that made him remarkably
accessible to spirit influences, and a fit instrument by
which the forces of the spirit world could act upon
men still in the body?

In the first place, Jesus of Nazareth belonged to a
race which was highly mediumistic from its beginning.   Abraham, the great founder of the Jewish
nation, could see spirits and hear spirit voices, and

he received many communications from the spirit world. Isaac also acted under spirit direction. Jacob was more mediumistic than Isaac, and in him the medial gifts of his grandfather were revived and perhaps increased. He saw angels going to heaven on a ladder and returning thence, he wrestled with a materialized spirit, and he became wealthy through spirit power. Joseph had a cup by which he divined, and "coming events cast their shadows before" for him, in his prophetic dreams. Moses was a really wonderful medium. In addition to the natural powers of his race, the laws of spirit communication known to the priests of Egypt were taught to him in his education at the Egyptian court. He was a great seer, and he recorded in Genesis his vision of the creation and the development of the world. He saw the successive stages of creation in a vision, and called these stages successive days, for they seemed to be days to him. His rod was so charged with magnetism that spirits who desired to free the Jews from Egyptian bondage brought on the plagues by means of this rod when wielded by Moses. The Red Sea was divided by the same power, and manna was materialized for their sustenance in the wilderness. David was an inspirational medium. All the old prophets spoke and prophesied under spirit influence, clear down to Malachi. Then for about four hundred years, this mediumistic power seems to have diminished, but it was revived in Jesus of Nazareth to an astonishing degree. In that superstitious age, when the powers of nature were but little understood, his deeds seemed miraculous, and a proof of his divine origin.

Jesus had a pure and healthful body. Being a Nazarene from his birth, he had never tasted fermented liquor. The poison of alcohol had never entered his body, to dull his brain, inflame his stomach, and interfere with the life processes of the tissues. Tobacco was then unknown, and the development of the mind and body of Jesus was not hindered by its use. Endowed with a magnificent and yet a very sensitive physique, he never debased it by the slightest sensuality. In him the mind was fully regnant over the body. He lived almost wholly out of doors; and his constant walking kept him close to nature, and in harmony with the magnetic currents of the earth. His mother was herself a medium, for she saw angels and talked with them. She was rarely spiritual, and drew the best sort of influences to herself. Jesus was her first-born son, and the rare gifts of Mary were transmitted to him in all their freshness and all their purity. His father Joseph was a good man. He was a man of action and courage, as well as accessible to spirit influence; for when a spirit warned him of danger to his first-born child, he started in the night for distant Egypt with his young wife and baby-boy.

Jesus was brought up in a pure, quiet, Jewish

home. He was bred to a trade, and his body was developed by healthful toil. As nothing is recorded of him between the ages of twelve and thirty, and as he gave many precepts akin to those of Buddha, some have inferred that he spent a portion of those eighteen years in India. Such may have been the case.

At any rate, on reaching the age of thirty, there he was in Judea, the purest, the most spiritual, and the most gloriously endowed man in the whole Roman Empire. His body was perfect; his mind was intuitional, clear, and strong; his spirit was courageous and true, and had the power of looking through all shams, down to the very root or core of every subject that was presented to him. And he was conscious of other powers of a spiritual nature that set him apart from other men. At thirty, all his powers, physical, mental, and spiritual, had reached their maturity; and the time came to him, as it comes to all, when he must decide what to do with his powers. To solve this vital question, he secluded himself in a lonely wilderness for nearly six weeks. He knew that he had rare powers of a spiritual nature. He was clairvoyant and clairaudiant. He was a medium through whom matter could be disintegrated and recomposed by spirits in the spirit-world. He was endowed with magnetic healing currents that sent new life through all with whom he came in contact. "What shall I do with all this?"

was the question that came to this wonderful scion of the Jewish race.   At last, worn by fasting, the temptation came to him to make a material and a selfish use of his powers.   He was very hungry, and stones could be turned into bread if he chose to use his mediumship in this way.   Wealth was clearly at the command of one who should develop his power in this direction.   Jesus did not so choose.   Shall he dazzle and astonish mankind by leaping from the topmost spire of the temple?   He knew he could do this feat with safety, for his attendant spirits were familiar with laws employed by spirits in our time, who raise pianos to the ceiling, and gently bring them down again.   But no: he will not debase his mediumship by trying to astonish the world by its exercise.

Another temptation came to him.   Milton calls the love of fame "the last infirmity of noble minds." Jesus, like all highly endowed men, had a desire to influence men and nations by his powers.   More wonderfully gifted than Gyges, the shepherd who reached a throne by the power of his magic ring, shall he aim to reach the summit of earthly power? Judea was then crushed under Rome.   Patriotism might well justify him in seeking to free his native land.   An execrable man, Tiberius, was emperor of Rome.   Abandoned to sensual pleasures, he was rioting on a distant island.   A corrupt prime minister was plotting against him in Rome.   Shall Jesus work on from point to point, till Tiberius himself be dethroned, and he, a Jew, hold the scepter of the Roman world? "No, no!" was his reply to these ambitious promptings.

Why did Jesus say no to such temptations? It was because he clearly saw, like Socrates and Plato, that this physical world is but the temporary shadow of eternal realities. He clearly saw that the *real* world is the unseen one, beyond the ken of the physical eye. Instead of using his great powers for temporary and shadowy good, he chose to use them for objects that have a permanent value. His decision was made to use his mediumship in order to lessen human misery, in order to teach men to build their permanent homes in spirit-land, in order to purify man, and to raise him to a more spiritual plane. Then and there, Jesus decided to mould his life according to the principles laid down in his unparalelled parable of the "Last Judgment." This is a story by which he illustrates the effect on our future state of kind and loving acts or those of an opposite character. It is no more to be taken literally than the illustration of the maidens who were going to the wedding feast, or of the servants to whom their master had entrusted his money, that are recorded by Matthew in the same chapter. In this fable of what men have called "The Last Judgment," Jesus simply taught that the kind and loving ones are fitted to go into bliss on leaving the body; while the

selfish and unloving will have to remain in an un-
happy condition for ages and ages.

Let us now consider some of the evidences of the
mediumistic powers of this man of Nazareth.   Let
us first call to mind the trinal nature of man, so far
as disembodied spirits have been able to analyze it
for us.   The most advanced spirits generally agree
that we now consist of physical body, spiritual body,
and soul.   With the organs of our physical body,
we become cognizant of, and we can affect, material
substances and organizations.   Some of the phases
of mediumship lie in the development of the senses of
the spiritual body.   In clairvoyance, the eyes of the
spiritual body are so developed that by them we can
see the spiritual bodies of spirits.   In clairaudiance,
the ears of our spiritual bodies can take cognizance
of sounds in spirit life.   The physical, or natural
body of Jesus (See 1 Cor. 15: 44) was perfect.
His spiritual body was also perfectly developed.
The spiritual garment of his soul was normally perfected.   He could therefore see spiritual realities
with his spiritual eyes, just as plainly as we see
physical things with our physical eyes.   Hence, he
knew the reality of the world of spirit.   His mediumship was perfect, natural, and normal.   Ours should
aim to be the same; and the time will come when
all men and women who will then dwell on the earth
plane will be just as cognizant of spirit life as Jesus
was.   He saw spirits and talked with them.

What were some of the other phases of his mediumship? He was probably the greatest healing medium that has ever walked the earth. And true to his resolution to relieve human suffering as far as possible, he exercised his healing powers more than any other spiritual phase. As Luke says, "Virtue went out from him, and healed them all." Many particular cases of his curing disease are recorded, and unnumbered cases are spoken of in the mass.

But this wonderful healing power of Jesus seems to have depended on certain conditions. It was necessary that the diseased person should believe in the power of Jesus to heal him. The accomplishment of the cure depended on two things: the power exerted through Jesus, and the confidence of the sick man in that power. Having assured himself that the sick man believed in his power, the healing spirits that used him as their instrument were able to pour the life-giving currents through him into the sufferer, and the diseased condition gave way to normal well-being.

If healing mediums of this day wish to attain the power of Jesus, they must try to attain those conditions under which he worked. Jesus had bodily vigor, inherited from pure parentage and from right habits of life. He lived much in the open air, he was perfectly pure and temperate regarding all the bodily appetites, he was totally indifferent to money-making, he lived for others and not for himself, and he relied wholly on the powers above him.   A medium in whom all these conditions are found can heal like Jesus.

He healed bodily ailments.   Crowds drew on his magnetic powers.   When so worn out that spirits could no longer act through him, he withdrew from the multitude to some solitary place.   On some mountain top, in some deep wood, heart to heart with Mother Nature, his powers were recuperated by the spirits with whom he communed, and he then entered new magnetic conditions in another village.

But he healed not only diseases of the physical body.   He also freed those who were under obsession of undeveloped spirits.   His pure strong personality could control such spirits, and his will-power forced them to leave their temporary abiding place. Many of the insane in our asylums are enthralled by undeveloped spirits who cling to the earth-plane. Well would it be for them if those in authority could allow pure mediums, who know how, to free these poor unfortunate victims.   Other conditions of insanity result from diseased conditions of the mere body, which temporarily hinder the mind from expressing itself.   Good magnetic mediums would aid such cases far more than doctors by the exhibition of drugs.   The inmates of insane hospitals will be greatly helped by increased knowledge of the laws of Spiritualism.

Did Jesus raise persons from the dead?   We

know that he did not, for he did not break the laws
of Nature. When the vital cord that unites the
spiritual body to its fleshly covering has been once
severed, it never unites again. The three cases of
raising from the dead by the Nazarene that the
church claims are those of the daughter of Jairus,
the widow of Nain's son, and Lazarus. In two of
these cases, Jesus said expressly that they were
asleep. See Luke 8:52 and John 11:11. Not one
of the three was dead at all. Each one was in a
trance sleep. The magnetic vitality of Jesus freed
them from this trance; and Elisha did the same for
the son of the Shunamite woman, as recorded in
2 Kings 4:33—36. The physicians of the time
thought they were dead. They sometimes think so
now, when the entranced person is in a trance sleep.
Irving Bishop was in such a trance; and when the
mistaken surgeons plunged their lancets into his vital organs, they caused the vital cord to part, that
in all probability was as yet intact.

Jesus, like many seers, could prophesy truly regarding the future. Spirits who are disembodied
can see causes and their ultimate results to better advantage than those who are hampered by physical
bonds. They communicate their foreknowledge,
which is based on the relations of existing facts, to
their mediums; and they thus enable them to prophesy, as Jesus and the ancient Hebrew prophets did.

His turning the water into wine and making of

bread are no more wonderful than the creation of
dewy flowers within closed slates.   This latter thing
has been actually done, under absolute test conditions, not once, but many, many times in the United
States during the past thirty years.   Great loaves
and hams and other edible articles have been either
made, or conveyed by spirits, to mediums under absolute test conditions.   Those who have seen a
chest with six men on it pushed across a room by
invisible power, and those who have seen a medium
carried out of a window and brought back again by
invisible hands, are not surprised to read that this
wonderful medium of Judea could walk on the
water without sinking.   If the spirits really stilled a
storm through the mediumship of Jesus, we cannot
claim, *as yet*, that this has been done of late.   But
as mediumship advances, it may be done in the future.   A hundred years ago, we could not have
made men think that a heavy train of cars could go
by the expansive force of invisible steam.   And ten
years ago, we did not believe that cars could be
propelled by the still more wierd and intangible
electricity.

Many who have not investigated spiritualism are
unable to believe that a piano can rise to a ceiling,
unsupported by any props.   But this has happened
many times.   Spirits tell us that they have learned
how to neutralize the power of gravitation, temporarily and within a limited space.   Intelligent and

scientific spirits who are freed from the body can do as wonderful things in spirit, as can Watt, and Morse, and Edison, in the body.

One of the wonders done by Jesus has been often paralleled by the materializing mediums. We refer to the transfiguration scene. This was not done in the presence of the multitude. On the top of a mountain, accompanied by the three most mediumistic disciples—Peter, James, and John—he was transfigured; and Moses and Elias, who had been in spirit life 1450 and 900 years, were materialized so that the three mediums saw them. Peter proposed then and there to make three cabinets, one for Jesus, and one for Moses and one for Elias, in order to retain these delightful conditions.

As to the resurrection of the physical body of Jesus, as claimed by the church, we object to it on the ground of materialism. We fail to see the use of a flesh body in spirit life. Moreover, if the cord that united his physical and his spiritual body were really severed, it could not be re-united without violating natural law. Of course, hanging on the cross a part of one day need not necessarily have caused the death of his body. But on the other hand, John, who was an eye-witness, says he was pierced in the heart with a spear, and a wound like that inevitably separates the spirit from the body.

We do not blame honest skeptics for saying that the body of Jesus, really dead, did not come to life

again. We say the same. But we, who have actually seen many temporary materializations of the
"dead," and many etherealizations of them, have no
difficulty whatever with the statement that Jesus was
seen and handled by the disciples after the body had
died.   These appearances were always in the presence of mediums. Peter, James, and John, the
strongest mediums, were generally present. The
appearances took place at night, or in the early
morning twilight. So the most favorable conditions,
as known to us, i. e. the presence of mediumistic
persons, and a subdued light, were presented on
these occasions. His first materialization was in the
early twilight, to Mary Magdalene. She was a
strong medium, and was at one time obsessed by
seven spirits, from whose tyranny she was freed by
Jesus. His last materialization was on a mountain
in Galilee, with eleven disciples present. Even on
that occasion, though all saw him and worshipped
him, *some doubted*. See Matt. 28: 17. So some in
our own day doubt spiritual manifestations. They
want to believe, but materialistic notions cling to
them, and make them doubt the evidence of their
own senses.

Jesus was a medium, or a mediator, in the truest,
purest sense. He was a medium between the physical world where we now dwell, and the spirit world.
His life was a beautiful and perfect one. His death
was pathetic, and even sublime, in its patient endur-

ance of terrible physical suffering.   No such trying circumstances attended the transition of Socrates. His death was painless, and only the sobs and tears of his friends marred the ease with which his spirit parted from the body.   Jesus, on the contrary, after a night of torment and insult, hung on a cross in the utmost bodily agony that that cruel age could devise. In excruciating pain, hounded by malicious enemies, and temporarily triumphed over by bad spirits, his faith in the future life held firm, and we rejoice to think that all this pain was at last *"finished."*

A matchless life! Let us imitate him in all. When his precepts are followed, and his life is imitated by all on the earth-plane, then will Spiritualism, pure and unadulterated, be the religion of the world.

TO HIS SOUL.

"Vital spark of Heavenly flame,
  Quit, oh! quit this mortal frame.
  Trembling, hoping, lingering, sighing,
  Oh! the pain, the bliss of dying!
  Cease, fond nature, cease thy strife,
  And let me languish into life.

"Hark! they whisper; angels say,
  'Sister spirit, come away.'
  What is this absorbs me quite,
  Steals my senses, shuts my sight,
  Drowns my spirit, draws my breath?
  Tell me, my soul, can this be death?

"The world recedes; it disappears;
  Heaven opens on my eyes; my ears
  With sounds seraphic ring;
  Lend, lend your wings. I mount! I fly!
  O grave, where is thy victory?
  O death, where is thy sting?"
                    —ALEXANDER POPE.

Pope wrote to his friend Steele in regard to the composition of this
poem, "It came to me the first moment I waked this morning."

LECTURE VIII.

In considering this subject, let us first seek to establish in our minds a clear notion of the meaning of
the word "religion." The derivation of the word
will aid us here. "Religion" is derived from "re,"
back, again, anew, and "legere," to gather what we
read, speak, and think; or "ligare," to bind. We prefer the latter derivation. According to this, religion
is that which binds us back, or again, to something
to which we really belong. The church would say
that religion is that which binds us back again to the
Supreme Being. In Raphæl's painting of "The
school of Athens," he has Plato stand with his hand
raised to heaven, in allusion to his doctrine that from
God everything is derived, and to God it will finally
return. This thought of Plato is a noble idealiza-
tion of the priestly view of religion. We Spiritualists accept that view in part, but we think that it
savors too much of theology, and does not sufficiently
emphasize the everlasting personality and individuality of the human soul. We add to the thought of
Plato, that religion, in its truest sense, is that which
binds the soul lovingly and indissolubly to all other

souls, whether individualized or absolute.   Our soul is now somewhat hampered in its expression by its physical clothing and material surroundings; and the religion of Spiritualism links us with sweet enthrallment to all embodied spirits, and especially to all disembodied spirit, or spirits, that pervade the universe. We say that it binds us especially to the disembodied, because, from their freer condition they can teach us things we cannot yet know for ourselves, and they can meet and aid our aspirations.   Religion surely fails of its mission, unless it tends to raise us to a higher spiritual plane.   It puts us then into vital connection with all progressive, aspirational souls; and, in its largest sense, this connection is inevitable with all such souls, be they freed from earth conditions, or still linked to the fleshly covering.

Before proceeding, we wish to point out that religion is to be distinguished from theology.   Religion is purely subjective, as it has to do with the relations that we as individual spirits sustain to the individual or collective spirits of the universe.   Each one's religion, then, is for himself alone.   Its satisfaction and its joy rest in the fact that it is the personal possession of the soul to whom it belongs. "A stranger doth not intermeddle with his joy." Theology, on the other hand, is objective.   It has to do with a being outside of one's self, a being whose attributes are carefully mapped out by those wise individuals, the theologians of the old school.   They define a personal being, and they give the name of God to this personality. They make him separate from those he created; and, having put him on a pedestal all by himself, they tell us to worship him. They think they know all about God, and they call this knowledge theology. This distinction between religion and theology explains the claim of many Spiritualists, that they do have a religion, while the true Spiritualist refuses to accept such a thing as theology.

Let us now go on to show that the same spiritual manifestations that form the basis of Spiritualism also form the foundation of all the religions of the world. And if it be shown that just such manifestations form the original foundation of the religion prevalent in this country, then the attempt which the church makes to put down Spiritualism, the very prop on which Christianity itself rests, will seem absurd to the last degree. It would be somewhat like a child sitting on his father's lap, who tries to upset the chair that supports his father. It is like a bird sitting on his nest, who tries to uproot the tree on which his nest is resting.

Now, how does a religion have its origin? We can conceive of two ways. What are they? One way may be that one man, or several men, put their reasoning powers together, think out what elements would be suitable for a new religion, and then form these elements into a system. The scheme being perfected, they then propose it to other persons, declare that they have adopted it as their own, and advise others to take it on the ground that it is a very good kind of a religion. How many persons would adopt a religion that was presented to them on such grounds? Would not those who were urged to join the new faith say, "You want me to believe such and such things. How do you *know* that these things are true? What proof can you give of their truth?" The originators of the new scheme will say that they have thought it out, have brought into the scheme what they think is true, and they point out the merits of the new religion. Those whom they are trying to convert will naturally say that if that is all the ground that they have to rest on, they can themselves go to work to make up a religion that will probably suit them better, as it will be the product of their own minds, and will therefore be better adapted to their own needs. When the early apostles asked men to accept Christianity, they did not ground the new religion on its being a coherent assemblage of good notions. They grounded it on certain spiritual manifestations made by the founder, some of which they could themselves reproduce. On account of these spiritual phenomena, they claimed that the new religion had a divine origin.

What is the other way in which a religion may originate? A man, or some men, find that under

certain conditions or at certain times, they fall into a
state during the continuance of which ideas come to
them regarding moral truth, or the Supreme Being,
or future events, or the nature of the world beyond
the grave, which do not come to ordinary men, nor
to themselves under ordinary conditions.   They are
themselves convinced that some outside force, that
some outside spiritual power takes hold of them,
and that they receive from this external spiritual
power, communications that are beyond the ability
of man to produce in and of himself.   On these
grounds, they adopt these religious views as the
truth; and, being true and of vital importance, they
wish to communicate them to other persons, so as
to induce them also to receive these views as the
truth.   In this way is the religion begun, and in
this way does it begin to spread.   Is it not probable that each religion of the world has had its origin in some such way as has just been described?

Of course those bigots who claim that their own
religion is the only true one, and that all who do
not adopt it will be damned forever, think that their
special religion was given to its originators by Almighty God himself.   This claim rests on the opinion that God has chosen out one nation from all the
rest, and that he has given to that nation the one
only true religion.   This notion is a very selfish
one.   It is indeed wicked, for it goes directly
against the truth that every human being derives

his individual existence from infinite life, that all are equally the offspring of that infinite source, and that all human beings are therefore brothers. Jesus formulated this glorious and comprehensive truth when he declared, "All ye are brethren: one is your Father." See Matthew 23: 8, 9.

Instead of so narrow and partial a view, is it not more than likely that the Infinite Source of individual life has seen fit in many different ages of the world, in many different nations, and under many varying circumstances, to come to persons who are more spiritual and more sensitive than ordinary men, and make them the vehicle of some great moral, or religious, or spiritual truth?

We said that the Infinite Source of being might see fit to do this. But is it likely that these truths are communicated directly, and without any finite instrumentality? We think it more probable that infinite being inspires these spiritual thoughts into sensitive human individuals, by and through individual finite spirits who once dwelt in the flesh as we do, but are now out of the physical body. This seems more than likely from the following considerations.

We see that infinite life in general produces its effects, not directly, but by the intervention of indirect means and instrumentalities. And these means and instruments, when organized, reach a higher development in the process of being thus employed.

The testimony of spirits also is all in this direction. They tell us that they are requested by higher powers to communicate spiritual truth to sensitive persons; and they also tell us that their work in this direction serves to further their own development. Besides, it is more natural that a finite individuality receive special impressions about some special thing from another finite individuality who is more advanced, than that it should receive them from infinity. The mother gives impressions to the child, the teacher instructs the pupil, the more advanced feeds the soul of those a little lower; and these natural processes obtain in the communication of spiritual food in all the universe. We are not now speaking of such à priori ideas as that of infinite space, of infinite time, and of an efficient cause. Those ideas, being innate, belong to the constitutional nature of soul existence, and do not need to be communicated, were it even possible to do so. We are speaking of those moral, religious, and spiritual truths that are definite, and form the basis of the religions. Infinite life works on and through all; but, all being "parts of one stupendous whole," the higher work on the lower, and the lower work on those who are lower than themselves. Thus all have their part to do, and they are enabled to do their part by the share of infinite life that pervades them.

There is another reason for thinking that the different religions of mankind came from individual

spirits, and not directly from the Infinite Source. It
is this.   If any one religion had come directly from
Almighty God, it would have all truth embodied in
it.   Bigots will make such a claim, each one for his
own system of belief.   But is this true of any one
religion?   Does any one faith have *all* truth?   We
find on the contrary that different religions have
different truths, and that all religions, even the lowest, have some truth.   This fact makes it probable
that each of them originated through the influence
on some sensitive brain of some exalted spirit or
spirits, who saw certain truths very clearly.   Rejoicing themselves in the truths they saw, they were
delighted to communicate them to their mediums.
But they did not communicate all truth, because being themselves finite, and therefore limited in view,
they were not able to see all truth.

Let us now consider a few of the great religions
of the world, and show that some kind of spiritual
manifestations forms the corner-stone of each.   The
originators or the upholders of these religions have
been under the influence, or, to use a common expression, under the "control" of some individual
spirit or spirits; and so what is really spiritualism
is the chief prop of each of them.   We shall try to
confine ourselves to those systems that have been
adopted by the largest number of people, or those
that were accepted by the most remarkable nations
in history.

Let us first consider the religion of ancient Greece. Though this was one of the smallest nations in territorial extent, yet Greece had, and continues to have to the present day, more influence on every form of literature, on art, on taste, and on philosophy, than any other nation that has ever existed. Though Rome triumphed over her materially and politically, the writers, the philosophers, and the artists of Rome never claimed to be more than imitators of the Greeks. Greek sculptors, Greek poets, and Greek orators were their models, and their highest aim was to resemble them. The authors of Greece lead in every department of writing. In philosophy, Plato and Socrates still lead, though Bacon has taught mankind to go far beyond the teachings of Aristotle, in studying the facts of physical nature, in order to apply its laws to the well-being of the human race.

The Greeks had acute, active, and practical minds. Their religion so impregnated their thought, that their writings can not be wholly understood without a knowledge of their mythology. While we know that their great philosophers gave in esoteric circles a meaning to the mythic tales that they hid from the multitude, yet the Greeks in general believed their religion, and made its teachings a part of their daily life. The main object of the great tragedies of Aeschylus, Sophocles, and Euripedes was to teach the principles of their faith to the common people of Greece. Their religion was not theoretical, as is much of the church doctrine of the present day. They prayed to their deities, offered them gifts, and depended on them to take care of them when they should leave the earth and go to Hades.

Now, on what did the Greeks rely as proofs that what their priests taught them was true? Every student of Greek history and literature knows that their faith rested directly on their oracles and their divinations. If their oracles were not to be depended on, then their religion had no proof Sophocles expresses this thought in one of the choral songs in Oedipus: "Never again will I adore the holy seat of Delphi, unless Phoebus' word be justified by clear fulfillment." Some shallow historians have spoken of the priests of Delphi as tricksters, and of the people who went to consult them as deluded ones. A wide reading of Greek literature by an unprejudiced mind shows that this people *did* believe what was told them by the oracles of Delphi and Dodona. And is it conceivable that this bright, active, practical people rested on a cheat? It was not only on religious matters that they consulted these shrines. They went to them on practical matters of daily life, of business, of politics. Generals went to Delphi before engaging in war. Even foreign kings came to this famous shrine, and offered magnificent gifts, in exchange for information regarding the result of their enterprises. Croesus of Lydia sent three times to this oracle, and the prophesy given proved true in each case.

Now, what gave this power of foretelling future events, to the shrine at Delphi? Its priestesses were spiritual mediums. They were sensitives; they went under spirit control. The spirits who influenced them, being out of the body, could see the action of existing causes better that those who came to consult, and so enabled these mediums to foretell future events. One can read in "The Hidden Way across the Threshold," by Dr. J. C. Street, a clear account of the mode of procedure at Delphi, when they wished to obtain a communication from the spirit-world. The priests were arranged in the form of a horse-shoe magnet, open towards the east and towards the shrine. A line connecting the ends of the magnet ran due north and south. The high priest was stationed at the center of the semi-circle. At the north, or positive end of the magnet, was placed the most negative priest. At the south, or negative end, was placed the most positive priest. The other priests were ranged in gradation of mediumistic power, from the ends, to where the high priest was placed. In front of the high priest the weakest priestess had her station. In front of her was placed a stronger one, and so on, the chief priestess being farthest front and nearest to the shrine. All these men and women were mediums. Woman having, on general principles, more perfectly mediumistic qualities than man, we are not surprised that the best interpreters of the spirit world were priestesses. The horse-shoe magnet of priests harmonized the magnetic currents, and concentrated them on the chief priestess. These arrangements were in accordance with the instructions of most advanced spirits at the present day, and we advise attention to the principles involved in these arrangements on the part of circles who assemble regularly in order to develop a special medium. We certainly advise the horse-shoe magnet, when that is their object, but there would be no objection to having men and women sit alternately. When the object is to develop one particular person, or to obtain manifestations through one medium, the persons present should certainly sit in a horse-shoe opening towards that individual. If a number of persons are together for the development of all, they should be arranged in a complete circle, with positive and negative persons alternating with each other.

The priests at Delphi seem to have understood these natural laws of spirit influence better than those of other shrines. At any rate, they applied them more systematically, and the results were so fine that Delphi was the favorite oracle.

The oracle of Trophonius was remarkable in that the person who sought counsel was his own medium. Having gone through certain rites, he descended by a ladder to the upper cave. The opening into the

lower cave was very narrow. If courageous
enough to go on, he lay down and put his feet into
the opening. A force, like the current of a rapid
river, then carried him down into the lower cave.
There, some became clairaudiant, and heard what
they wished to know; while others became clairvoyant, and saw a vision. Some who went through
this experience never smiled again. This process
at Trophonius, though discredited by the ignorant,
will be understood by all who have had experience
as mediums.

The priests of these ancient oracles were evidently
Spiritualists. They knew the laws of spirit control
and spirit communications. It is evident that the
Greeks would not have relied on their oracles, if
those oracles had not proved true. They might
have depended on them a few times to begin with,
but when they failed to give true answers, their
faith in them would have waned, and at last have
completely died away. But we find that the influence of the oracle at Delphi continued for many
hundred years. It was consulted in fact for more
than a thousand years, and seemed at last to give
place to the new Spiritualism taught by the Nazarene. But while it lasted it was considered of the
greatest value by the Greeks. In fact, the Am-
phictyonic Council had for its main object the pro-
tection of the oracle at Delphi.

Egypt, too, had its oracles, the most famous one

being located at the oasis of Ammon.   The Greeks learned these great natural laws from the Egyptian priests, to whom this spiritualistic lore was handed down by the inhabitants of the sunk continent of Atlantis.

Another great religion founded on Spiritualism is Mohammedanism. Its founder, Mohammed, became an individualized entity about 569 A. D., and made his transition to purely spiritual life in 632.   What was Mohammed?   Was he an impostor, as some materialistic historians would have us believe? Coming to his death hour, his words were, "I come now to my companions on high."   These sublime words harmonize with a conscientious life, conscious communion with spirits, and an assurance that he was about to join them.   Such words in the supreme hour of transit befit a Confucius, a Socrates, a Lincoln.   They do not befit an impostor. His wife Cadijah, whom he married from friendship and gratitude, was the first to believe in his divine mission.   She who knew him best knew that he was sincere.   Mohammed was a trance medium.   Historians ignorant of the laws of spirit control believe that he had epileptic fits.   Students of the new biology know that he went under spirit influence. After long solitary vigils, he shouted, foamed at the mouth, heard musical bells ringing, heard voices, and spoke what he heard. These words were written down by his followers, and form the Koran.

He taught good precepts to the Arabs among whom he dwelt. He found most of them idolaters, and he taught them to substitute the worship of one spirit God. He found them drunkards and gluttons. He bade them abstain wholly from wine, and to eat but little during forty days of each year. He taught them to purify their bodies by a daily bath, and to keep in relation to the spirit world by praying to God five times a day. Familiar with Judaic and Christian teaching, he incorporated much of it in his precepts. But the founder of Christianity had been in spirit life six hundred years. His teachings had not penetrated Arabia to any extent, and Mohammed claimed that his own teachings superseded those of Jesus. The precepts of the Nazarene had been so distorted during those six hundred years, that we can hardly blame the spirit guides of Mohammed for claiming that their medium had brought a more perfect revelation to mankind.

Mohammed was a grand man, in both private and public life. He was abstemious in all respects. He was faithful to his aged Cadijah as long as she lived. When she left earth, he married a beautiful young woman. When this Ayesha, in the pride of youthful beauty, said to him, "Am I not better than Cadijah?" "By God, no," said Mohammed. "Never did God give me a better. When I was pronounced a liar, she believed in me."

The faith of Mohammed seems to be well adapt-

ed to western Asia and to Africa.   It is now
spreading with great rapidity in the latter continent.
It is estimated that there are ten converts to Mohammedanism in the newly opened regions, to one
convert to Christianity.   Christian bigots have little
notion of the power and the adaptability of its tenets to men just emerging from barbarism.   Its belief in one God, instead of three, and its precepts of
cleanliness and abstinence produce better results
than European rum and profligacy.

Brahminism, which was introduced into India by
the Aryans, had the Aryanic mill-stone of a personal god around its neck.   Uniting with the creator
Brahm the destructive Siva of the aboriginal race,
and the much incarnated Vishnu of the Puranas, the
religion of Hindostan became a monstrous cult which
has never spread to any extent beyond that country.   The pure and simple Buddha revolted from
the gross teachings of Brahminism, and formulated
a system that is followed by about a third of the inhabitants of the earth.   This man lived in the seventh century before Christ.   Lofty spirits, pained
by some of the features of Brahminism, found in
Buddha a fit instrument through whom to give
purer doctrines to the world.   Brought up in lux-
ury, he abandoned it for a life of austerity.   Still
unsatisfied and longing for more spirituality, he secluded himself for years, and at last became a perfect medium for spirit forces.   What did those pur-

ified intelligences teach him? They taught him self-denial, purity, kindness to all beings, both men and the lower animals. They taught him that the condition of man in spirit life will depend solely on Karma, that is, on the merit and demerit of his own actions. Buddhism is a beautiful faith, and bears a somewhat similar relation to Brahminism, that Christianity does to Judaism. Like Jesus, Buddha was ideally benevolent. His precepts embody the best Christian virtues. In one respect, however, this great religion is inferior to Spiritualism. The final absorption of pure souls into the Deity is repugnant to the grander views of our destiny that the spirit world teaches us to-day. More advanced now than when they taught Buddha 2600 years ago, spirits give us the ecstatic knowledge that our existence, having once been individualized from the fountain of infinite life, will maintain its individuality forever. Fear not to live, timid soul. Never will you lose your memory of the past. Never will you lose your identity. On the contrary, your individuality will develop, and the ecstacy of conscious being will irradiate your immortal life. Buddha knows this now, and rejoices in the knowledge.

The pure teachings of Buddha, expelled from Hindostan, spread rapidly to the east. It took different forms in different countries. In Thibet, it became Lamaism, a cult that has some spiritualistic features. In China, Buddhism holds its own by the

side of the other two religions adopted by 400,000,-
000 Chinese.   These two religions are that taught
by Confucius, himself a Spiritualist; and Taoism, the
religion of reason, and one that embodies some of the
features of Spiritualism.   Confucius taught his followers to do right, because their arisen ancestors
were with them, and saw all that they did.

Buddhism, Confucianism, and Taoism stand side
by side in China.   The men of China have a large-
ness of view that should put Christian nations to
shame.   When strangers meet in China and the
conversation turns to religion, they inquire of each
other, "Which of the sublime religions is yours?"
Instead of trying to proselyte each other, it is good
form for each to praise the religion of the others as
better than his own.   These compliments ended,
they all join hands, and unite in repeating the formula, "Religions are many, reason is one, we are all
brothers." *

The general population of China is not to be
judged by those coast-dwellers who seek their
fortune on foreign shores.   The Chinese are a
practical people, and their morals are good.   Licentious novels having been introduced by "Christian"
nations, nearly half a century ago, sixty-five book-
sellers in Soo Chow went together to the city temple and made a vow not to engage in the sale of

---

* See "Chinese Empire," in Chambers' Encyclopedia.

these books. Can this act be paralleled in any Christian city? In the name of all good spirits, do not let us carry fire-water, and opium, and licentious novels to vast peoples who do not have them.

The religion of the American aborigines is a Spiritualism suited to their stage of advancement. Their medicine-men were mediums. They worshipped, not idols, but the Great Spirit. On leaving the body, they passed to the happy hunting-grounds of the Spirit-land. No white usurper can drive them thence!

We have spoken elsewhere of the fact that all the great writers of the Bible were inspirational mediums, and that Jesus himself was the most remarkable medium between the earth and the spirit world on record. Moses was obeyed because of the spirit power manifested through him. The Judges of Israel ruled in the same way. The prophets were heeded because decarnated spirits spoke through them. Christianity was directly based on "spiritual manifestations" made by the Nazarene and his followers. This power continued among the believers for hundreds of years. When it ceased, the church became corrupt and formal.

Now what shall we say of those who fight Spiritualism with weapons drawn from the Old Testament? Is the Old Testament true? The only proof that any of it is true is the Spiritualism in it. Moses forbade all wizards but himself. He preferred to be the only one.   He did not want a "mixture of influences."

As to the remarkable power manifested by the pure Nazarene, let all mediums study the four gospels, and see what kind of a medium Jesus was. Let them try to do just as he did, and be just what he was, and then they will become endowed with the same loving and glorious power.

> " So low is grandeur to our dust,
>   So close is God to man,
>   When Duty whispers low, " Thou must,'
>   All can reply, 'I can.' "

THE PETRIFIED FERN.

" In a valley, centuries ago,
   Grew a little fern-leaf, green and slender,
   Veining delicate, and fibres tender,
Waving when the wind crept down so low.
Rushes tall, and moss, and grass grew round it,
Playful sunbeams darted in and found it,
Drops of dew stole in by night, and crowned it;
But no feet of man e'er trod that way,—
Earth was young and keeping holiday.

" Monster fishes swam the silent main,
   Stately forests waved their giant branches,
   Mountains hurled their snowy avalanches,
Mammoth creatures stalked across the plain;
Nature reveled in grand mysteries,—
But the little fern was none of these,
Did not number with the hills and trees;
Only grew and waved its wild, sweet way;
No one came to note it day by day.

" Earth, one time, put on a frolic mood,
   Heaved the rocks and changed the mighty motion
   Of the deep, strong currents of the ocean,
Moved the plain, and shook the haughty wood,
Crushed the little fern in soft, moist clay,—
Covered it and hid it safe away.
O the changes! O life! bitter cost
Since that useless little fern was lost!

" *Useless? Lost?* There came a thoughtful man
   Searching nature's secrets, far and deep;
   From a fissure in a rocky steep
He withdrew a stone, o'er which there ran
Fairy pencilings, a quaint design,
Veinings, leafage, fibres clear and fine,
And the fern's life lay in every line!
So, I think, God hides some souls away,
Sweetly to surprise us in Heaven's day."
          —MARY L. BOLLES BRANCH.

LECTURE IX.

HOW TO INVESTIGATE SPIRITUALISM.

There are many subjects for human beings to investigate, and they are led to these various subjects by many different motives. Curiosity is a powerful spur in pushing one's inquiries.

For many hundred years men have felt a deep cnriosity regarding the sources of the Nile, and the interior of Africa. To penetrate the secrets of the Dark Continent, many explorers have spent their money, wasted their health, and used unremitting toil and diligence. An anxious wish to solve the unknown has driven men to leave the temperate regions and plunge into the dreary realms of eternal ice. They wanted to find out whether there were land or water at the North Pole. They wanted to know if one could sail from Behring's Straits to the coast of Greenland. Sir John Franklin and many another man has left his bones to whiten under an Arctic sky. So eager were they to prove that navigable water borders the northern coast of Asia and America that they were willing to lay down their lives rather than give up the quest.

And yet, was it curiosity alone that led these gallant bands? Other motives had their share. Ambition to accomplish what no other man had done spurred them on.

What were the first words of Greeley to the rescuers that found him dying of hunger, cold and pain? "Greeley, is this you?" "Yes: did what I came to do—beat the best record," said he, and fell back exhausted. To get one mile nearer to the Pole than any one else was a triumph that paid him for many an agony.

A desire to add to the fund of scientific truth has also led on many an investigator. Once it was thought that the laws of science had to do only with our life while in the body. In accordance with this view, religious souls thought it almost wrong to devote any part of life's short span to scientific pursuits. They thought it better to devote one's self to Biblical and theological stndy. But the world is beginning to understand that scientific laws govern the spirit life as well as the present, and that all the knowledge we can obtain here will be useful to us in the vaster sphere which will soon be our home. The laws of what we call Nature prevail in all the universe, and the study of them acquires a dignity and a value that they did not possess before Spiritualism broadened the scope of human thought.

But there is a yet higher motive to the investigation of the unknown than curiosity, ambition, or the love of scientific truth. A desire to relieve suffering humanity, and thus link our being in the golden chain of love that binds all spirits together, is a yet higher motive.   It was all these motives combined, especially that of lessening the sum of human misery, that led David Livingstone through the pathless deserts of Africa.   To put an end to the horrible traffic in slaves, carried on by the Portuguese traders, was his eager desire.   Traveling through the African wilds, he often met bands of captives that were being forced to go to the coast.   Torn from their home and loved ones, suffering acute pangs of hopeless home-sickness, they were also treated with great physical brutality by those who expected to make money by selling them when they should reach the ocean.   They were forced to walk the hundreds of miles yoked in the following way, as described by Livingstone.   A trunk of a tree, with two forked branches, was prepared for each male captive.   His neck was put in the fork and riveted there by a staple.   Two such logs, to each of which a slave was fastened, were then tied securely together.   The two could not get apart, and the weight of the logs made the captives secure.   Those who could sustain the journey brought a good price at the coast.   Those who sunk were not released by these inhuman traders, and perished miserably in the wilds.   Livingstone's heart was wrung by sometimes coming to the dead bodies of captives still harnessed to the cruel yoke.   He relates that often when he met these forlorn bands, their wild singing had a note of triumph in it. Knowing somewhat of their language, he knew the meaning of the chant. The poor creatures were singing how when their souls should be freed from the body, they would come back and haunt their cruel oppressors, and thus repay their tyranny. Livingstone could take no rest while this "open sore," as he called it, remained. He loved those poor blacks, and did all he could to help them. This motive, to relieve human pain, so brightly displayed in the career of Livingstone and of Jesus, is the highest motive of any we have named. It is angelic. Our arisen angels, once subject to the pains we feel, stoop from their happy homes to help us. Do we wish to be like them? Then let us help all whom we meet in every possible way. Thus will the spiritual part of us grow and expand. Thus shall we aid the grand object of all good spirits—the progression of each and all. The love of science is good. But when science becomes the hand-maid of benevolence, she is helping the angel world in their great mission.

These four motives of curiosity, ambition, love of science, and desire to help other beings, are active in many of the investigations we make. In investigating Spiritualism, we find that men are spurred by the same, but let us remember that the desire to relieve the pain and to increase the happiness of other beings is the most angelic one.

Now, are many persons investigating Spiritualism? We do not wish to exaggerate, but we believe that the majority of persons we meet in daily life are investigating this subject. And of the minority who are not investigating it, a large portion desire to look into it, but are temporarily deterred from doing so. And, can there be anything more natural than this desire? What human being does not feel an interest in the coming years of this life? Whether he will be well, whether he will be happy, interests him greatly. And, if there be any possible way for him to *know* whether he will live after his body dies, and whether his dear ones who have already "died" are still alive, and love him still, then he cannot help taking a deep interest in the subject. The world has been told by the clergy for many hundred years that there was no possible way for us to know anything about the condition of the "dead," and that it was even wicked to think much about it. And now we meet persons every day who claim to have had communications from the "dead," who claim to have proof that their dear ones are alive, and love them still. How is it possible for persons to help taking an interest in this matter? How is it possible to keep them from investigating it? Men eagerly investigate all matters pertaining to the present life. And they will investigate this subject, the most interesting, and also the most important, that can possibly engage the attention of any human being. If

the husband, whose dear one has been torn from his
life, can learn for a surety that she is alive and
happy and loves him still, he will try to find it out.
The mother who has lost her idol will do the same.
All whose mothers are in spirit land will ask, "Is
mother near me? Can she come to me and care
for me with a mother's undying love?" If we *can*
know these things, we certainly *will* know them,
and the clergy cannot frighten us out of it. They
have told us that we can selfishly enjoy heaven,
while those we love are in misery in hell. They
have tried to crush the family feeling, and the love
that binds friend to friend. The world is learning
that the family tie will continue, that love does last
beyond the grave. Spiritualism can turn these
hopes into glorious realities. *We must and we will
investigate Spiritualism.*

Well, as most persons will certainly investigate
Spiritualism who have an opportunity of doing so,
let us seek to know the best methods of carrying on
these inquiries. We should surely use our reason
in this most important quest.

Suppose a man wishes to look into the subject of
electricity. Does he begin to practice experiments,
and use the electric forces, before he has learned
anything about their laws? Would it not be dangerous to do so? Would he not run the risk of sepa-
rating his spirit from his physical body? And if
care and study are requisite in investigating electric

and magnetic forces, when they concern only material objects, how much more study and care are
befitting, when these forces are used by disembodied
spirits in order to communicate their thoughts to us
in the flesh!   Only careful study will teach us to
apply conditions that will make such communications possible and beneficial.   A man who wishes
to make use of electricity knows that he must begin
at the first principles of the science, and master
them thoroughly.   Then having learned the A, B,
and C, he can go on step by step and work to advantage.   What do we think of a man who sits
down to a telegraphic machine, knowing nothing of
its working, with a message that he expects to send
to Boston, and to which he wishes an immediate
reply?   He does not understand the laws of electricity, nor their application to the machine before
him.   He makes no connections.   He sits there,
expecting his message to go to Boston, and to receive an answer to it.   Getting no response, he begins to feel somewhat annoyed.   "Well," says he,
"I will give this machine one good trial.   If I don't
get an answer from Boston, then I shall know that
telegraphy is a fraud."   He waits awhile in impa-
tience.   No message comes.   He leaves the instrument in disgust; and for weeks he tells telegraphic
operators of his acquaintance that he has investigated the machine, that he has positive proofs that it is
a fraud, and that people are fools to think that they

can get a message from Boston by any such means.
The men who know the laws of electricity hint that
perhaps he did not make the connections right, and
that there was some scientific cause for the failure.
But he insists that this talk of "connections" and
"conditions" is designed to cover the incapacity of
the instrument, the fraud of its operators, and the
deluded state of those whom they fool. "I have
investigated it," he insists, "and the thing is a humbug." What do we think of such a man? And
yet, have we not known persons who have attended
a few séances, who applied none of the proper conditions of investigation, and who then declare that
they have looked into Spiritualism, and have found
out that it is a gigantic fraud?

Some, still more foolish, decide the value of its
claims without looking into it at all. On no grounds
whatever, they say that Spiritualism is false. Is the
reason, is the power of judging from facts, to be
misused in this way? The same want of method in
mental processes would make a man say that the
Congo river does not have a horse-shoe bend in it,
because he had not seen it; and that Stanley is a
humbug, because he did not accompany him in his
wonderful journey through "Darkest Africa." Bacon told us to examine facts, and find out laws and
principles from those facts. His method has accomplished wonders in two hundred and fifty years in
earth investigations. Many in this age are wise

enough to apply his method to psychical and spiritual investigations, and the progress made is very gratifying to those who are prepared to accept the truth in these new fields of inquiry.

What are the conditions of a right investigation of Spiritualism? Let us first consider the mental attitude of those who investigate. Our illustration of the man who could get nothing by the telegraphic machine may help us here. Why did he not succeed? He did not try to understand the laws on which its action is based, he was dictatorial, and he was impatient. What qualities befit the successful seeker into any realm of science and thought? There should be close and persistent study, a docile and unprejudiced frame of mind, a desire to know the truth, the whole truth, and nothing but the truth, and, leavening the whole, a patient spirit. These qualities imbue a Morse, a Newton, an Edison, and also the most successful investigators into the means of communicating with the spirit world. A few efforts are not enough. Many, many efforts must be made.

> "If at first you don't succeed,
> Try, try *again*."

The seeker should look to his motives, and strive to be guided by the highest. If he is investigating just in the hope of developing a power that will enable him to give psychometric readings, or séances, at one dollar a head, his motive is a selfish one, and he will draw selfish spirits to his aid. If he develop the power desired, this class of spirits may help him to make money, and he may succeed for a time, in a business way; but he thus excludes a higher grade of spirits, and will enter the spirit world as crippled as though he had not called himself a Spiritualist. If his motive be to astonish and dazzle the world by the display of remarkable gifts, he will draw to him those who manifest selfishness by their ambition. Spirits who desire to spiritualize mankind will seek another medium of communication.

The bodily condition of the investigators, especially those conditions that depend on their own habits of life, should be considered. All who drink alcohol, all who are steeped in tobacco, those who are intemperate in eating, and all who are licentious in act or in thought should be rigorously excluded from the circle of honest investigators. There is danger in sitting with any such. The reason is psychologic. Spirits who were addicted to such vices when on earth and have not yet progressed out of those conditions are naturally drawn to those who practise the indulgences they formerly enjoyed. They creep within the magnetic sphere of such, solace themselves in the old sensual delights, and become a detriment to the pure seekers. These spirits will stimulate the sensual human beings, so *their* investigations into Spiritualism will not help them. "First pure," said the brother of the Nazarene. See James 3:17. The old proverb, "Like attracts like," is true of all spirit relations, and is never more applicable than in all our attempts to communicate with the spirit world. To draw the seraphic, rather than the undeveloped spirits, the seeker must be filled with the divine wisdom that is "pure, peaceable, gentle and easy to be entreated, full of mercy and good fruits, without partiality and without hypocrisy." Divine wisdom, as above delineated, will unlock the door into the higher spiritual realms. Indissolubly wedded to this wisdom is divine love, which links all souls together, be they high or low.

A sound physical condition in those who sit is an advantage. Health facilitates the smooth flow of a magnetism that is in harmony with the terrestrial currents, and those currents are the vehicle used by our spirit friends in giving us their thoughts. Hence, it has been said that no person suffering from a chronic disease should be allowed to sit in a "circle." But, dear friends, let us not forget the divine, unselfish love just alluded to. If a circle of pure persons, in good physical condition, do sometimes admit a diseased one, they could no doubt greatly benefit such a one. And the unselfish love thus manifested would aid them spiritually to a degree that would more than compensate for the slight and temporary lessening of their own vital strength.

What has been said of the mental attitude, the

motives, the purity, and the physical condition of
the investigators, applies of course with yet greater
weight to those who have already become what we
call "mediums." If mediums possessing these desirable qualities be not at hand, it is better to sit
without one. Persistent and regular sittings
may in time develop a good medium in the circle.
And if a person be so situated that he or she can
find no suitable persons with whom to sit, we think
it would be far better for him to sit alone. True,
that person may never in earth life develop into a
strong medium. But the very effort will advance
him spiritually. We advise one so situated to try to
take a half hour two or three times a week, on regular days and hours, if possible. Let him sit quietly,
in a restful position, freeing his mind as far as may
be from his worldly cares. Let him lift his soul to
the great Source of life, and to the loving dear ones
who have left the body. Let him invoke their aid,
and invite their spiritual presence. Such aspirational hours will prepare him to profit by more favorable circumstances that may yet be developed in his
outer life. And even if the hoped-for opportunities
never come to him in his earth life, these aspirations for a purer, more spiritual life will prepare
him for that glad hour when the dear friends beyond
will welcome his spirit as it leaves the poor, toil-
worn body, and show him the shining way to the
everlasting spirit-home.

In connection with the general subject of this lecture, let us now consider briefly some of the qualities that specially befit those who desire to be good mediums between mortals and those who are already in the spirit life.   A medium, literally, is something between two spaces, or two states, through which action, motion, or thought is transmitted.   Its perfection will depend of course on the transmission's being effected with as little change as possible in whatever is conveyed.   For instance, the glass in a window is the medium through which we see the world outside of the house.   If the glass be perfectly transparent, we see the outside objects just as they are.   If the glass be flawed, we see the objects distorted from their true form; if the glass be muddy, we see them indistinctly; if the glass be colored, we see them in that color.   A good medium, spiritualistically speaking, then, is a person through whom the thoughts, the words, and the sights of the spirit world can be conveyed with but little change by the transition.   And through a perfect medium, were such a one possible, the impressions of the spirit world would be conveyed to mortals exactly as they are.   Transparency, then, is the most desirable quality in a spiritual medium.   This transparency comes about in two ways.   The medium may be very simple and very negative by nature.   He has no positive qualities that color and distort by his own opinions and prejudices what the spirit world attempt

to convey through his instrumentality. Or, he may
be a person so constituted and so trained that he
can, when he chooses, so efface his own will and individuality as to allow the impression to pass through
him without being altered.   In addition to this mental quality, he must have that physical constitution
of body that will enable spirits to use his organism
in one or more of the phases of mediumship.
Whether he possess those qualities can be known
only by experiment, or by the statement of some
experienced spirit specially skilled in the wonderful
science of communicating with us in the body.

Some investigators fall into the error of thinking
that any or all of their spirit friends can come to
them through any good medium.   The truth is that
all spirits, in the body or out of the body, have their
own magnetic aura, and these varying aura cannot
assimilate with all.   All spirits cannot come through
all mediums, though probably all spirits can communicate through some medium somewhere.   Certain of your spirit friends, for instance, come through
a medium.   You call him or her a good medium,
and you tell a friend about it.   He goes to the same
person, gets nothing, and thinks he must be a fraud.
Let us go to different mediums, whom we believe to
be honest, and we shall in time receive communications from some spirit that will satisfy us.

Many who embrace Spiritualism and are made
happy in knowing that the dead are alive and can

still communicate with us, make the mistake of
thinking that any of their friends can come at any
time, through any medium.   After a while they are
disappointed to find that this is not so.   Their dis-
appointment sometimes reacts on their interest, and
they begin to fear that it is all a mistake.   But patient, persistent, and thoughtful efforts will lead us
in time into a clearer view of the relation of things.

While in the body, our main care should be to
try to unfold the soul.   On leaving the body, that is
still our main care; and the more advanced a spirit
becomes, the more clearly does he see this great
duty, and the more earnestly does he work in order
to aid that unfoldment.   The occupations of life in
the spirit world are many, and adapted to the tastes,
the nature, and the degree of unfoldment of those
who dwell there.   A portion of them are specially
engaged in improving and practising the ways of
communicating with those yet in the body.   They
are particularly adapted to this work.   But many
of our spirit friends are engaged in occupations
quite different from this.   When they wish to exchange thoughts with the dear ones left behind, they
go to one of these specialists in the art of communicating with mortals, somewhat as we go to a tele-
graph operator, or as we ask an adept in finger
language to talk for us with a deaf and dumb man.
A clear apprehension and acceptance of this fact will
save those who enter these paths from many a dis-

appointment.   Let us apply this view to some of the common phases of mediumship.

You sit down to a table with a rapping medium. His controls have learned by long practice to manipulate his magnetism, so that they can produce tips or raps by it at the precise instant they desire. Your spirit friend is close by, and signifies to the spirit adept what answers he wishes to be given to your questions.   You remain passive, and your own magnetism may assist in assimilating the magnetism of the two spirits, and thus aid the result.   If you persevere in sitting at the table, you may in time develop your own powers in this direction, and you may find a spirit friend who will become skilled in using your magnetism in this way.   Your own dearest spirit friend may become an adept in this method of communications, and may make you happy by doing so, until the laws of spiritual unfoldment require him to cease this work in order to go up higher.

Suppose you go to an independent slate-writing medium.   His "control" has learned to so use certain elements of his organism that he can produce writing on the slate, provided that his medium be in connection with the slate.   This spirit adept does the writing in nearly every case.   Our friend in spirit is near by, and tells him what to write.   The searcher who expects to get the *hand-writing* of his spirit friend expects what cannot be obtained, unless that spirit friend be both an adept in this means of communicating, and can also manipulate the organism of this special medium.

Take the wonderful art of spirit photography. Not all spirits have learned how to express their form in that special way that can impress the plate in the camera. When we go to have our "spirit picture" taken, it is most unlikely that the one whose picture we most desire is an adept in this line, and can present his picture on our plate. For this reason, many are disappointed in their experiment. "Do you *recognize* any of the faces on your picture? "No," is the doleful answer in almost every case. And yet there are true spirit pictures with your own. If possible, the spirit control has a presentation made of some who have been connected with you at some period of life. If that be not possible, good spirits who know how to be taken present themselves, and it is a true spirit picture, though you be not able to recognize them.

But the most disappointing of all the phases, that is, at its present stage of development, is that of materialization. As materialization becomes better understood, and is lifted out of the unreasonable into the possible, it will become a yet grander proof to skeptics of the truth of Spiritualism than it has been in the past. The great error is that of thinking that *all* spirits have learned how to materialize so as to be recognized. The truth of the case is that but few spirits are adepts in this wonderful art. The spirit controls of a materializing medium, understanding the scientific laws pertaining to this form of manifestation, have experimented with his organism, he being in a trance, until they have learned how to draw from him and from those present the elements which they make into a materialized form. This form is artificial, and is temporarily made up by the spirit adepts. These cabinet controls enter this form, or they aid other spirits to enter it. Our spirit friend has a task whose subtle difficulty we are not in condition to fully appreciate. One spirit friend, when questioned as to past facts, said, "I cannot tell. You know I am not *all* Alice" (giving her own name). That spirit must temporarily inhabit that form, hold it together with the assistance of the cabinet controls, remember how his body used to look and make this form look as he used to look in earth life. And, as if all this were not enough to do at one time, his earth friend draws from his power by a suspicious attitude of mind. He regards him as an impostor, and demands dates, and names, and facts, that may "test" that he is not a humbug. So difficult is this task that it is probable that the forms at a materializing séance are often manipulated by one of the cabinet controls. Our spirit friend is close by, tells the control how he used to look and what he must say, and the control represents the loving, anxious spirit friend as well as he can.

When materialization assumes its proper place, people will understand that the actual presentation of their own friends does not always occur; and that the formation and dematerialization in a good light of any spirit whatever who can move and talk will be one of the best methods of demonstrating spirit existence to a materialist. Such a demonstration was made to me, as described in the Fourth Lecture. I have attended over sixty materializing séances, with five different mediums, thirty-five of them being with the medium through whom the aforesaid "George" demonstrated his spiritual existence. And yet, in all those sixty séances, I did not see many manifestations that could *force* conviction on a skeptic. The reasons are not far to seek. Those who frequent séances expect too much, in that they all expect to have their own spirit friends. The manager keeps the room very dark, because light uses up the materializing power so rapidly that a form cannot be produced for each person in a large company, if it be very light. Each person pays a dollar; and, the more persons present, the greater the pecuniary proceeds. We are not now speaking of those mediums who eke out genuine materializing power by the aid of soft white blankets, wigs, veils, and other paraphernalia. We are speaking of the natural results, with ordinary good mediums, of the mistaken notions of sitters and of the desire to make money-making subordinate to the advancement of Spiritualism.

Well, what in general should be our main objects in investigating Spiritualism? A desire to communicate with dear ones in spirit life is natural and right. But that should not be our final aim. A still higher object is the development of our own spirituality, so that we may be better fitted for the next life. And when to these we add the desire to reduce human suffering, by bringing news of loved departed ones to the mourner, and by removing the fear of death, we are then working in complete harmony with higher spirits, for we are then working for human progress. Helping others in love will make us live in heaven while here in the body, and we thus become links in the glorious chain of love that binds all finite souls together. And this love, ever increasing, ever progressing, will forever raise all finite souls to the infinite Source of all love and light and life.

IN MEMORIAM.

The following letter is by the poet Tennyson, and is dated Farringford, Freshwater, Isle of Wight, May 7, 1874. It was written to a gentleman who communicated to him certain strange experiences he had had when passing from under the effect of anesthetics. Tennyson writes:

"I have never had any revelations through anesthetics, but a kind of waking trance (this for lack of a better name) I have frequently had, quite up from boyhood, when I had been all alone. This has often come upon me through repeating my own name to myself silently until all at once, as it were, out of the intensity of the consciousness of individuality the individuality itself seemed to dissolve and fade away into boundless being, and this not a confused state, but the clearest of the clearest, the *surest of the surest*, utterly beyond words, where death was an almost laughable impossibility, the loss of personality (if so it were,) seeming no extinction, but the only true life."

This is the most emphatic declaration that the spirit of the writer is capable of transferring itself into another existence that is not only real, clear, simple, but that it. is also infinite in vision and eternal in duration.

It is pointed out by Prof. Thomas Davidson, who has seen the letter, that the same conviction, if not the same experience, only with another, is described in "In Memoriam."—*From the Chicago Tribune.*

" By night we linger'd on the lawn,
  For under foot the herb was dry;
  And genial warmth; and o'er the sky
  The silvery haze of summer drawn;

" While now we sang old songs that peal'd
  From knoll to knoll, where, couch'd at ease,
  The white kine glimmer'd, and the trees
  Laid their dark arms about the field.

" But when the others, one by one,
  Withdrew themselves from me and night,
  And in the house light after light
  Went out, and I was all alone,

" A hunger seized my heart; I read
 Of that glad year that once had been,
 In those fall'n leaves which kept their green,
The noble letters of the dead:

" And strangely on the silence broke
 The silent-speaking words, and strange
 Was love's dumb cry defying change
To test his worth; and strangely spoke

" The faith, the vigor, bold to dwell
 On doubts that drive the coward back,
 And keen thro' wordy snares to track
Suggestion to her inmost cell.

" So word by word, and line by line,
 The dead man touch'd me from the past,
 And all at once it seem'd at last
His living soul was flashed on mine,

" And mine in his was wound, and whirl'd
 About empyreal heights of thought,
 And came on that *which is*, and caught
The deep pulsations of the world,

" *Æonian music* measuring out
 The steps of Time, the shocks of Chance,
 The blows of Death.   At length my trance
Was cancell'd, stricken through with doubt.

" Vague words! but ah, how hard to frame
 In matter-moulded forms of speech,
 Or ev'n for intellect to reach
Thro' memory that which I became.

" Till now the doubtful dusk reveal'd
 The knoll once more where, couched at ease,
 The white kine glimmer'd, and the trees
Laid their dark arms about the field."

LECTURE X.

Is death real, or is it imaginary? Spiritualists are said to claim that there is no such thing as death, and we often quote with delight Longfellow's beautiful lines:

"There is no death; what seems so is transition."

Still, there is such a thing as death. But a Spiritualist differs from some other persons in applying the term death very closely to only one part of the triple nature of a human being while on the earth-plane. To a materialist, whether confessedly or only unconsciously one, death is indeed death, for he thinks it means the total and final extinction of a human being, when the earth body falls into dust. Such must be the belief of an actual materialist. But this doctrine is so repugnant to our nature that those who do not really know of a life beyond the death of the material body, either by revelation or by Spiritualism, prefer to call themselves Agnostics. Like the friends of Socrates, to whom no spirit was able to manifest itself as his attendant spirit did to him, they think there is some reason to believe that

199

the spirit may survive the death of the body. They
hope it may be so, but they do not actually *know*.
One part of his nature being not yet completely developed, Robert Ingersoll, so clear-headed, so noble-
hearted, so patriotic, is at present an agnostic as to
a future life. But in his case, it will take but a
short experience in spirit life to bring him into the
clear light of knowledge. That inexpressibly sad
and doubtful woman, George Eliot, who said, "Let
us be very kind to one another, for to-morrow we
die," sank into the depths of agnosticism. The
philosphical and conscientious John Stewart Mill
could not, while here, feel sure of the continuity of
life. In his agnosticism, we see the natural rebound
of a sensitive and ideal nature, which had been
cramped in its development by the narrow processes
to which it had been subjected by a bigoted father.
Because the elder Mill was narrow and fanatical,
though earnest and sincere, he tried to bind his son's
soul by the same shackles. But the psyche could
not be held in chains, and the rebound that came in
middle life made John Stuart Mill an agnostic. Had
he known something definite of the spiritual philosophy, had its sweet light dawned on him, he might
have been a Spiritualist. Many of his thoughts and
opinions trend that way. His essay on "Liberty"
shows that he was prepared to do justice to the
spiritualistic conception of individuality. And his
essay against the "Subjection of Woman" shows

that his logic did not blind him to the value of intu-
ition.   But the great sad heart of Mill broke when
his idolized wife left him.   Let us quote some of
the words he placed on her tombstone at Avignon.
After summing up her noble traits of character, he
says, "Were there more like her, this earth would
already become the hoped-for heaven."   He hoped
there was a heaven for his Harriet in spirit land,
but—he did not *know*.   But a little while, and they
laid his worn-out body beside hers, and the great
agnostic entered on the knowledge of what he had
longed for.   Let us thank Infinite Love that Mill
and his wife, and brave George Eliot now know the
ecstasy of continued being, wholly freed from the
uncertainty that perplexed them while in the body.

Well, what is death?   And, in what way, and
with what limitations may the term ever be applied
to the experiences of a human being?   In other
words, is there any part of us, in our present condition, that is subject to death?   To answer this question, we will first consider what death is, and after
that we will note the constitution of a human being
while he is still on the earth plane.

Death is the total and the permanent cessation of
all the vital functions in an animal or a vegetable
body.   Why do these functions cease?   They cease
because the life, whatever that may be, has gone
out of this organic body.   Of course as thinking
Spiritualists we claim that generic or universal life

is everywhere, and that nothing would be at all, were it not for this pervasive life. So, when we say that an animal or vegetable body is dead because the life has gone out of it, we mean of course that the special, individualized, organized portion of the universal life, which vitalized that special body so that it could perform its own individual functions, as an animal or a vegetable, has gone out of it. When this particular life has gone out of the organism, the physical body remains, and is subject to the natural laws of physical substance. In accordance with these laws, the body gradually disintegrates into its original chemical elements, and these freed elements are now ready to enter into new combinations in plants and animals.

The word death is applicable then to the physical bodies of men, animals, and vegetables. It applies to their material bodies, but not to the individualized spiritual life of them, which ascends to its own place in the spirit-world. The word death, we say, applies to all these physical organisms. But there are other words, nearly synonymous with death, that mankind in general apply to human beings alone. Among these words are decease, demise exit, release, and departure. These words of course involve the notion that the human being whose life once filled that physical body has gone away elsewhere. The word death is Anglo-Saxon. All the other words cited are derived directly or in-

directly from the Latin language. We would expect the uncivilized Saxons, not yet developed from
the material notions that pertain to the earliest
stages of man, to apply the word death indiscrimin-
ately to men and animals.   But the cultured ancient
nations of Southern Europe well knew that when a
man "died" his immaterial part did not cease to be,
but went away somewhere else.   The pagan Emperor Hadrian gracefully expressed this belief in his
lines beginning, "Animula, vagula, blandula," where
he says to his own soul,

> " Roving, charming, little soul,
>   The guest and the companion of the body,
>   Into what strange places are you now going,
>   Cold, pallid, naked little thing?
>   You do not jest now, as you used to do. "

This notion of the separate existence of the soul
has been entertained by all advanced nations.   It
seemed almost new to the Jews of the time of Jesus,
on account of the materialistic condition into which
that nation had fallen, during the four hundred
years after the death of Malachi.   Many of us feel
that we owe a debt of gratitude to the Christian
church for keeping alive a belief in the continuity of
spirit life after the death of the body.   But the
church conception of spirit life is erroneous, limited,
and material.   Some of its features are so repulsive
that thousands have fled to even materialism as being preferable.   Now that the glorious light of
Spiritualism has taken away what was wrong, lim-

ited, and material from the church notion of life in the spirit world, we earnestly hope that all may grasp these newly revealed truths. We do not however wish these reasonable views of spirit life to enter the church creeds in combination with all the other errors that find expression there. Can we believe in an amalgamation between truth and error? On the contrary, let those persons still in the church who have secretly embraced Spiritualism and are trying to wed its free teachings with "orthodox" doctrines, come bravely and truly out of the church. In other words, let them leave all errors, and receive the truth, the whole truth, and nothing but the truth.

Our second point of inquiry is the constitution of a human being while on the earth plane. Knowing that, we shall know which part, if any, is subject to death, and which parts are not subject to death in earthly conditions.

Man, in this present earth condition, so far as we are able to formulate what we cannot now clearly comprehend, is three-fold, and is constituted of physical body, spirit body, and soul. A familiar illustration proves the present existence of the spirit body. Persons who have lost a limb feel pains and discomfort in that limb just as if it were still joined to the body. In fact, the limb of the spirit body is still connected. Cases are familiar of maimed persons whose limb felt cramped and suffering until the

severed member was taken out of some small box
or uncomfortable position. Paul made the same
three-fold division when he spoke of "our whole
body, soul, and spirit," though he used a somewhat
different wording.

The physical body is what we see now, and know
the appearance of each other by. Like other organisms, it is mainly composed of carbon, hydrogen,
oxygen, and nitrogen. This part of us is perishable;
and when life leaves it, it disintegrates into its original elements, and loses its individuality. The spiritual body permeates the physical body, and enables
it to perform its functions. The same thing is done,
imperfectly and temporarily, by spirits who enter
the form that is seen at a materializing séance. It
was probably through such a materialized form that
the spirit of Jesus manifested itself to the disciples
after his dissolution. We all have a spiritual body,
and it resembles our physical body. This resemblance will enable us to recognize each other after
we shall have entered spirit life. This spirit body
can be developed while we live on the earth. This
unfoldment depends on right living, feeling, and
thinking. The better it be developed while we are
in earth life, the better equipped shall we be on entering the Spirit-world. This spirit body does not
perish, when the physical body perishes. Within
the spirit body is the soul, which is a vital spark
from the fire of infinite being, a drop from the fount-

ain of infinite life.   The spirit body is as individual
as the physical body.   So far as we now see, the
soul within has become individualized, and will retain
its identity and self-consciousness forever.   It lives
and moves and has its being in infinite life, and yet
it possesses and rejoices in its individual entity.
This derived, separate, and yet dependent existence
of an individual soul is the most wonderful thing in
the universe.   The unfoldment of this soul should
be our main object here, and it engages and will engage the attention of all progressive beings in the
Spirit-world.

On this foundation of the three-fold nature of man,
we say that "death" is the separation of the imperishable spirit-body and soul from the perishable
physical body.   When this takes place, what is left?
The dead physical body, the corpse.   It is still dear
to those who loved the being who once inhabited it,
but the life having gone it is destined soon to decay,
and must be quickly disposed of.

This separation of the spirit body from the earthly
body is really our second birth, and is what Jesus
alluded to in John 3: 5.   God being spirit, Jesus
sought to make Nicodemus see that he would not
enter the kingdom of spirit until he should be born
again.   When we enter the Spirit-world, we can
apprehend spirit and spiritual things to a degree
that is now impossible.   In our first birth, we
emerge from the safe, comfortable, but circum-

scribed resting-place in the bosom of our mother, into a new world. We were alive there, but that life was narrow, and we would not wish to return to it. By and by, we shall be born the second time. As before, we pass from a narrow, circumscribed life into a freer, brighter life; and, as before, we would not wish to return to the previous straitened existence.

Clairvoyance has cast a new and glorious light on what is called death. A clairvoyant person is one in whom the eyes of the spirit body have been so developed that, though still in the physical body, he can see the spirit bodies of those in spirit life, and many other features of that existence. This is one of the most beautiful and desirable phases of mediumship, and should be earnestly cultivated by those who can obtain it. It was possessed by many of the early Christians and is called "discerning of spirits" in 1 Cor. 12: 10. Persons who sometimes see waves of light, when they quietly repose in darkness, possess the germ of this most satisfactory power. It was increased, in the case of the writer, by putting herself habitually in harmony with the magnetic currents of the earth.*

After the advent of Modern Spiritualism had revived this glorious clairvoyant power, it began to be hoped that persons thus gifted could really see

---

* A work on this subject, giving full particulars and directions, will be published later by the author of this book.

the separation of the spirit from the body, and tell the world the actual meaning of the word "death." We believe that Andrew Jackson Davis was one of the first to see the transition from earth life to spirit life, and he has written a minute account of what he saw. This separation of the arising spirit from the fleshly tabernacle has been seen many times by persons in the clairvoyant state, and has been frequently described. We will recapitulate the main features of what takes place.

What does the clairvoyant see? Over the body of the dying person, he sees a light cloud form and thicken. As the lower limbs become cold, this cloud gathers towards the vital parts of the body, This process continues until the light cloud, having become more dense and firm, assumes a globular shape, and hovers over the head of the dying one. This globe of light is connected with the top of the head (the organ of veneration or spirituality, and the part that retains the vital heat the longest) by a slender cord that looks like silver. After a time, this globe of light begins to assume the form and features of the person when in earth life. He looks the same, except that he looks smaller, more refined, and more beautiful. Around this form, the clairvoyant sees loving spirits, the friends of the new-comer into spirit life, who are aiding the process and receiving the new-born one. When perfectly formed, the cord separates, and the happy spirit, being now lighter than the air, easily ascends in company with his rejoicing friends, who show him the way to his new spirit home.   George MacDonald has beautifully remarked that the happy smile so often seen on the face of the dead is the last impress made by the vanishing psyche as she sees the bliss into which she is entering.   "How happy he looks!" we sometimes murmur, as we look on the face of a dead friend.   *No wonder that he looks happy!*

With regard to that silvery electric cord, Mr. Davis says that though it separates, a small portion of electricity remains with the body.   He says that it is owing to this that disintegration does not take place instantly.   This merciful provison gives time for the loving, tender rites of those who love that dead house of clay.

But, does Spiritualism give us any information that may serve the interests of our friends who are about to leave this life?   Communicating spirits tell us much in this connection that we wish to know.

In the first place, those who love the dying one should try to facilitate the inevitable departure rather than to prevent it.   The psychic power of reluctant friends makes it hard for the spirit to be freed from the body.   Some of us remember how in Mrs. Browning's "Isobel's Child," the dying babe begs its mother to loose her prayer.   "It bindeth me, it holdeth me," sighs the little one.

The most truly loving friends are the unselfish

ones who repress their sobs and unavailing entreat-
ies, and in gentle quietude let the departing soul free
smoothly and without hindrance from the toil-worn
body.   Going as he is to old friends and to another
and more beautiful life, let us not break in on the
coming rupture by sounds of lamentation and agonies of supplication.   If our *letting* them go enables
them to go more happily, let us forget ourselves,
and maintain a conduct that will permit the scenes
of earth to fade gently into the glory of the spirit
life!   The faces of dear ones gone before hover
over the enraptured gaze of him who is about to
join them.

A dear friend whose only child, a beautiful girl
of sixteen, was borne away to spirit-life, has one
consoling memory of those last sad days.   The
mother had a sister in the spirit world whom the
child had never seen, but whose name she had often
heard.   The last two days of her earth life the
young girl was unconscious much of the time.
When she aroused, and saw her mother tenderly
ministering to her, she would say, "Oh! I thought
it was aunt ——," naming the aunt she had never
known.   Her mother has the comforting knowledge
that her darling child was learning to know that
dear relative while still in the body, and the assurance that she went peacefully to her new home in
her tender care.

And does Spiritualism tell us how to dispose of

the deserted body, in a way to favor the interests of
the arisen spirit? It does give us valuable information on this important point. A full enjoyment of
the freedom of spirit life cannot be attained till the
old physical body has begun to resolve into its original elements. Hence, it is unwise to put the body
on ice, or to embalm it. These attempts to retard
the disintegration of the body tend to hold the spirit
in earth conditions. We suppose that the best
method of all, so far as the ascended spirit is concerned, is that of placing the body on a platform up
in some lofty tree, as was practiced by some of the
Indian tribes. The spirit can hover near, as the
body passes into its original elements, and the arisen
one gradually and easily becomes acquainted with
its new mode of life and new means of locomotion.

Under the present conditions of civilized life, with
the earth becoming more densely populated from
day to day, we find that advanced spirits strongly
advise the cremation of the body. Some who had
been cremated have described their sensations in
spirit. Of course they were conscious of no pain.
The speedy separation into the original elements by
the action of fire completely emancipated the spirit
from all physical conditions. This was effected so
quickly that these spirits testify that they came very
suddenly into a blaze of light that almost dazed them.
They soon became accustomed to it, however, and

speak strongly in favor of this method of disposing of the abandoned earth-house.

So the welfare of the dead, as well as of the living, is promoted by the burning of the bodies of the dead. Spiritualism here, as elsewhere, is in accord with the views of the best scientists of the day. Burning the bodies of the dead burns up all those tiny unwelcome guests whose harborage has, in most cases of disease, expelled the original and lawful tenant. By shortening the period of his earth life, they have deprived him of the share of physical existence that was his due. It is probable that the deleterious bacilli and microbes come from the "fermentation," described by Mr. Hiram E. Butler, in his "Seven Creative Principles," and we shall not object to seeing them "transmuted" by fire. The spirit world advocates cremation because the destruction of the germs of disease promotes physical health and so prolongs life. They understand better than we do that we enter spirit life better equipped by having had the full measure of earth experience; and that whatever shortens life here detracts from our complete development.

Recurring to what clairvoyants have seen at the time a spirit is freed from the body, we are reminded of the experience of a lady who knew very little of Spiritualism. Her little daughter four years of age lay at the point of death. She was her only child, and her agony at losing her darling seemed

beyond endurance.   In feeble health herself, she
thought she could not survive the loss of her little
girl.   She gazed despairingly at her idol, and knew
that the moment of separation was near.   Suddenly,
the walls of the room seemed to have disappeared.
She saw the beautiful blue sky strewn with white
fleecy clouds.   Amid the clouds was a large company of little children.   Stretching out their hands
towards her little girl, with beckoning gestures and
happy smiles they seemed to ask her to join them.
Then she saw her darling rise from the bed, stretching out her little arms to that rejoicing company.
Her dress was pure white, her yellow curls floated
behind her.   Laughing joyfully, she floated up, up,
till she joined those other children, and they all
went together into the fleecy clouds up in the blue
sky.   The sky disappeared, the mother saw again
the walls of her room, and the body of her little
girl lay on the bed, but the spirit was not there.
This comforting vision showed the mother that her
darling still lived, and that she had gone with loving little ones to a beautiful home.   Her sorrow
was deep indeed, but there was an element of con-
solation, instead of stony despair, from this glorious
glimpse into the Spirit-world.   . Later, she sometimes heard the merry laugh and the word "Mama"
in tender tones.   The bright presence is gone from
her daily life, but she *knows* that her precious one

still lives, and that sometime, she will clasp her
again, no more to part.

Is this view of death simple and beautiful?   It is
more than beautiful: *it is true.*

Entering on spirit life is not a resurrection.   That
word means a rising *again,* a resumption of life.
When we "die," we do not cease to live for awhile,
and then begin to live again.   Not at all.   We go
on living.   The only part of us that ever knew anything at all is more alive than ever, for it no longer
has the body to impede its activity.   Those who
cling to the old doctrine of the resurrection think
that the body of Jesus came to life again, and that
it lived again.   This doctrine is a materialistic one.
The teachings of Spiritualism have gradually
leavened these old notions, so that many "orthodox"
ministers are now declaring that what the disciples
saw after the burial of their master was his glorified
body, and not his previous physical body.   What
became of that physical body, they do not presume
to say.   Some advanced spirits tell us that the
Nazarene belonged to the brotherhood of the Es-
senes, and that some of the "brethren" carried the
body away and buried it in secrecy.   Whether that
be so or not, Spiritualists know well that if his body
really died, it never lived again; and that what the
disciples saw in the upper room at Jerusalem, by the
Sea of Galilee, and on the mount of ascension, was a
temporary materialization of their arisen teacher.

Science, unenlightened by the facts of Spiritualism, is unable to tell us what death is. Herbert Spencer says life is "The definite combination of heterogeneous changes, both simultaneous and successive, in correspondence with external co-existences and sequences." According to this, in death this "definite combination" comes to an end. This definition is excellent, so far as it applies to the merely physical part of us. But Herbert Spencer does not tell us what becomes of the "real, thinking, feeling man," when his physical body disintegrates. He has done noble work in systematizing the evolution theory. His mental labors have been mostly in the direction of our present earth life. His great, clear mind seeks the truth. It is possible that full illumination may not come to him in earth life. But, once freed from physical chains, no spirit will enter on its immortal heritage with more conscious joy than will this great thinker of our time.

The unsolved mystery that has puzzled philosophers has been cleared up by Modern Spiritualism. In "death," so called, the spirit body is born out of the physical body into a freer life. This we know, though what that new life will be, we cannot conceive perfectly until we experience it. Some speculative minds ask whether we may not be destined to be born again into a yet more ethereal state, after a certain experience in spirit-life. Shall we not, they say, find after awhile that our constitution there has more elements than the spirit body and the soul that we now think of as forming our being after leaving the physical body? Shall we not, in time, discard another outward shell, and enter a still more spiritual existence? This thought is finely treated of in that remarkable poem, "Face to Face," written by Paul Hamilton Payne, just before his transition into spirit life. This bright glimpse into future possibilities was vouchsafed to him in an inspired hour, and accords well with that eternal progression which is the most precious dower of every spirit. Thus is the king of terrors himself transfigured into a glorious and beloved angel by the Ithuriel touch of Modern Spiritualism. Milton pictures the unknown horror of death in a grand figure:

> " Black it stood as night,
> Fierce as ten furies, terrible as hell,
> And shook a dreadful dart: what seemed his head
> The likeness of a kingly crown had on."

Another writer alludes to "the coming bulk of death." This fearful monster, more fearful because we knew not what he was, is now shorn of his terrors. What we used to call death is now the open door into a new, immortal, and yet a natural life. Loved faces will bend over us, their familiar handclasp will greet us, the long departed father and mother will enfold us in their embrace. They will lead us up the shining pathway. They will teach us what we would know. We shall in time learn to speak the spirit language, by which all spirits can communicate with each other. We shall always love the memory of the earth, for it was there that we began to live.

With such a glorious prospect before us, can we not bear patiently the pains and losses of this fleeting earth life? Every care, patiently borne; every temptation of the lower nature, bravely conquered; every unselfish act, every true word, every loving smile will develop our spiritual nature here, and make yet whiter the robes we shall wear there. Our friends in spirit may know what we are doing. All our acts here re-act on our condition there. Let these incentives influence our daily conduct, and let us live for the glorious life awaiting us in the Spirit-world!

FACE TO FACE.

The following poem, probably the best of its kind in the language, was written by Paul Hamilton Hayne shortly before his death. "I wish the world to know," he said, "that this is my view of death, as a dying man."

" Sad mortal! couldst thou but know
    What truly it means to die,
The wings of thy soul would glow,
    And the hopes of thy heart beat high;
Thou wouldst turn from the sceptical schools
    And laugh their jargon to scorn,
As the babble of midnight fools,
    Ere the morning of truth be born;
But I, earth's madness above,
    In a kingdom of stormless breath—
I gaze on the glory of love
    In the unveiled face of death.

"I tell thee, his face is fair
    As the moon-bow's amber rings,
And the gleam in his unbound hair,
    Like the flush of a thousand springs;
His smile is the fathomless beam
    Of the star-shine's sacred light,
When the summers of Southland dream
    In the lap of the holy Night;
For I, earth's blindness above,
    In a kingdom of tranquil breath—
I gaze on the marvel of love
    In the unveiled face of Death.

"In his eyes a heaven there dwells—
    But they hold few mysteries now—
And his pity for earth's farewells
    Half furrows that shining brow;
Souls taken from time's cold tide
    He folds to his fostering breast,

And the tears of their grief are dried
  Ere they enter the courts of rest:
And still, earth's madness above,
  In a kingdom of stormless breath—
I gaze on a light that is love
  In the unveiled face of Death.

"Through the splendor of stars impearled
  In the glow of their far-off grace,
He is soaring world by world,
  With the souls in his strong embrace;
Lone ethers, unstirred by a wind,
  At the passage of Death grow sweet
With the fragrance that floats behind
  The flash of his winged retreat;
And I, earth's madness above,
  'Mid a kingdom of peaceful breath,
Have gazed on the lustre of love
  In the unveiled face of Death.

"But beyond the stars and the sun
  I can follow him still on his way,
Till the pearl-white gates are won
  In the calm of the central day.
For the voices of fond acclaim
  Thrill down from the place of souls,
As Death with a touch like flame,
  Uncloses the goal of goals:
And from heavens of heavens above
  God speaketh with tranquil breath—
My angel of perfect love
  Is the angel men call Death!"

LECTURE XI.

In all ages and among all races of mankind, when men have thought of existence after death, they have wondered where they were to be. Were they to "wing their flight from star to star;" or, being spirit, were they to be wholly destitute of existence in space at all? The various mythologies have given varied opinions on this point. The sun-loving, happy Greek had a very sad notion of life after the death of the body. Destitute of all covering, the souls even of the good were to go below the surface of the earth. There in Hades, with no sun nor moon nor star, they were to while away existence, longing forevermore to revisit the dear sun-illumined earth. Only a very few mortals, specially favored by the gods, were not subject to death, and went to dwell in the Elysian Fields west of the earth, beyond the ocean.

The Hindoo, Scandinavian, and Mohammedan abodes of the dead were not located in any accordance with modern astronomical or geologic science. The happy hunting grounds of the American Indians give a natural and reasonable notion of what would be heaven to them; and, as we shall see further on, accord with the true nature and locality of the spirit-world.

When we turn to the Hebrew Scriptures, we do not find any more reasonable notions of the spirit world than those given by the other religions. As to the Old Testament, that maintains a nearly total silence on even the continuance of life after the death of the body. How gloomy are the words of even the wise Solomon in Ecclesiastes 9: 5, "The living know that they shall die: but the dead know not anything." He also says in verse ten of the same chapter, "There is no work, nor knowledge, nor wisdom, in the grave, whither thou goest." Solomon, though the Christian church claim that his words were inspired by Almighty God, seems to have been an agnostic and a positivist of the most pronounced type. We think that those who decry the skepticism of John Stuart Mill and Huxley better amend their Bibles and leave out the book of Ecclesiastes.

So uncertain was the Jew regarding a world beyond the grave that the teachings of the spiritual Nazarene were indeed a new revelation to him. Jesus never claimed to raise a person from the dead into the life of this world, but he was ever conscious of a life beyond and outside of this physical existence. Spirits attended him in his hours of solitude. When he was hanging on the cruel cross, from which he

knew that death alone could free him, he had certain fore-knowledge of the coming spirit-life. He
said to the thief who suffered by his side, that that
same day he would be with him in a pleasant park;
for the Greek word "paradeisos," which he used,
simply meant a most beautiful pleasure-garden. He
was fully aware that this thief, who had a kindly,
loving nature, and that he himself, whose sole aim
was to be good, would be in a very pleasant place
as soon as their souls could get out of their suffering
bodies. He used to tell his disciples that there
were many mansions in the world beyond, and
that he would personally prepare them for them, if
they were only faithful to what he had taught them.

But a great many years after Jesus had passed
into spirit life, when the good John was nearly a
hundred years old, he was confined a prisoner on a
lonely little island. There he passed into a trance
state, and had very vivid visions of scenes beyond
our daily life. But his visions of the beyond were
colored by his own mental constitution and religious
prejudices. Being always a Jew, the heaven that
John saw was of course a new Jerusalem, a spiritual
revival of the old capital of his nation. Not long
ago, we heard Mr. Hull speak of this conception of
heaven by John. He remarked that as gold was
then esteemed beyond all natural beauty, John covered the streets of the city with that metal; while
the present notion of heaven would be that we would

tread on flowers. Yes: instead of gates of pearl
and walls of precious stones, the heaven we know
of will have no walls at all, and the little children
will run about everywhere, and we shall have all the
most exquisite flowers ever dreamed of by a poor
invalid in a crowded city hospital.   John's heaven, a
solid cube, walled in and covered with gold, accorded
with the notions of his time, but it does not accord
with what is taught us by Modern Spiritualism.

It will not of course be expected that man should
be able to locate the spirit-world, while the ancient
erroneous notions of the earth and the heavenly
bodies prevailed. To the primeval man, the earth
was a flat plain, warmed and lighted by a fiery ball
that passed at regular periods over it, and also lighted by other balls or spots of light that took their
course with more or less regularity.   As the reason
of man grew, an innate idea of an efficient cause of
each effect led him to query what the flat plain
rested on.   Some of the old mythologies told him
that it rested on the coils of a great serpent.   If he
ventured to ask what held the serpent up, probably
the priests told him that was a mystery, and that
something dreadful was sure to happen to him, if he
should try to find out what was meant to be hidden
from human vision.   Modern clergymen have met
in the same way the question how a finite being can
at the same time be an infinite being.   But the human mind is no longer in its babyhood.   It can no

longer be hushed to sleep by a childish nursery song.

In course of time, the absolute regularity in the motions of some of those bright spots in the sky arrested attention. They made practical, everyday use of some of these phenomena, and the science of astronomy began. But many, many hundred years passed before man was able to seize upon the true relation between this great solid earth, and those brilliant lights overhead. They were used for "signs and for seasons, and for days and years." Little did they think that some of these spots of light were far bulkier than the earth they trod upon. Moses described them and their creation according to the crude notions of astronomy that prevailed in his time. An acceptance of this fact gives a complete key to the harmony between what *seemed* to Moses and what is *known* to modern astronomers and geologists. Those who are interested in pursuing this thought are referred to Boardman's "Creative Week," a work written in the interests of the church, and yet pregnant with much that is true, and redolent with real spirituality.

We alluded a few paragraphs back to John's notion of a cubical heaven, measuring fifteen hundred miles each way. That this notion of John was considered a mere vision by the Christian church, and not to be taken literally, is proved by its accepting Dante's representation of hell, purgatory, and heaven. In fact, Dante took many of the theories preached in the churches in his day, and welded them into one harmonious, though mistaken whole. His conception, though narrow and erroneous, is deeply interesting to the student of astronomy, for it shows the progress the world had made toward the truth since Ptolemy taught in Alexandria in the second century after Christ.

Dante, who was born in 1265, places the beginning of his journey into spirit-life in the year 1300. He was familiar with all the learning and all the philosophical speculations of his time. Those who think that everybody believed the earth was a flat plain and that the heavenly bodies moved around it, until Kepler gave the true plan of the solar system and Galileo proved it by his little telescope, have an incorrect view. Little by little did the true system of the universe creep into the mind of man. Three hundred years before Galileo, Dante presented a scheme of the spirit world that approximated the truth. He evidently did not believe the earth was a flat plain, for he places the mountain of Purgatory in a great ocean on the other side of the world.

We will recapitulate his plan of the spirit world, pointing out the truth and the error of its astronomical features. Like Homer and Virgil, he makes hell below the surface of the earth. It is therefore unlighted by sun, moon, or star. He makes hell consist of nine circles, each one smaller and deeper than the preceding, and he places the ninth or lowest

circle exactly in the center of the earth.   He places
the entrance to the uppermost circle of hell not far
from Jerusalem.   Occasionally in going down he
meets rivers that had their origin on the surface
of the earth.   These special rivers flow downward;
and, as there is nothing to prevent their doing so,
their waters gravitate to the center of the earth.
That Dante thought of the earth as a globe, with
an attractive power at its center which acted equally
in all directions, is evident from the disposition he
makes of Satan.   Those who had taken their own
lives or the lives of others by violence were placed
in the seventh circle.   Those who had deceived
were placed far below the violent, in the eighth circle.   And away below the eighth circle, at the center
of the earth, are the traitors, who combined murder
with fraud.   At the central point, Satan the arch-
traitor is placed.   Now comes the proof that Dante
was well aware of a center of gravity that acted
equally in every direction.   He and his guide Virgil creep down the gigantic body of Satan, until
they reach the center of his body, at the center of
the earth.   At that point, instead of climbing down,
they are suddenly obliged to reverse their own bodies completely; and, as they go along the legs of
Satan towards his feet, they are forced to climb up.
They continue climbing until in process of ascending
they at last reach the other side of the world and
"again behold the stars."

We now come to a superstitious absurdity, which the great poet mingles with much that we may call wise, and even scientific—for the fourteenth century. He gives us to understand that when Deity threw Satan from heaven he struck the earth feet first. His impetus carried him to the center of the earth, where gravitation held him fast. But his immense bulk displaced an immense amount of earth substance, and so the mount purgatory was pushed out from the ocean on the other side of the world from where Satan struck the earth. Well, on this mountain are the seven circles of purgatory, and on its summit is the Terrestrial Paradise.

We see then that he located hell and purgatory wholly on or within this earth. Where does Dante place the third part of spirit-existence—Heaven? If he had made the earth a plain, lighted by brilliant dots of light, he would have had no place for heaven. But he evidently thought of the heavenly bodies as worlds like our own, for it is in these different worlds that he places the nine spheres of heaven. And yet, the successive arrangement of these heavens shows that he was very ignorant on two points. He did not know accurately the relative position of these heavenly bodies, and he had no conception of their relative size. We will name his heavens in their order, and the errors in his arrangement will be evident. His first heaven is located in the moon; the second, in Mercury; the third, in

Venus; the fourth, in the sun; the fifth, in Mars; the sixth, in Jupiter; the seventh, in Saturn; the eighth, in the stars Castor and Pollux; and the ninth, at the center of the universe, where the trinal nature of the Deity is manifested by the three primary colors. This last point shows that even Newton's theory of the composition of light was not quite unknown to the philosophic Dante.

Of course in this delineation of Dante's plan, we have not alluded to his theology, nor to the horrible misrepresentation of Divine justice that he perpetrates in discribing the tortures of his hell. To quote Mr. Ingersoll, like some modern churches he made God "an eternal jailer, without the pardoning power." We have simply given the astronomical bearings of Dante's scheme.

The main error in his plan is that all these heavens are made for man alone. One is led to inquire, "Where is the heaven of the inhabitants of Saturn, for instance, if Saturn is only one of the heavens for the good of this earth?" We have, however, no fault to find with his plan of hell and heaven, for it is in accordance with the imperfect notions of the solar system that belonged to the fourteenth century. His heavens are far in advance of the heaven described by John about twelve hundred years before. He is not to blame for his horrible distortion of infinite life into a cruel and vengeful demon, for he heard these wicked notions proclaimed in the church of which he was a most devout member.

Let us now see what effect the laws of Kepler and the telescope of Galileo had on the conceptions of the church, as voiced by the genius of Milton. What was Milton's plan of the universe? We will present it as clearly and as concisely as possible.

While it is true that Galileo's little instrument had not been able to give to the world the enormous dimensions of heavenly bodies and their inconceivable distances from each other, as modern telescopes have enabled astronomers of our day to do, yet in Milton's time, the relations of the members of the solar system were well understood. We shall therefore find none of the crude errors that Dante fell into. Milton's plan was a grand one, and worthy of his genius.

He considers that all that is, is embraced in a sphere with an infinite radius. Half this sphere is heaven, a region of light, beauty, and happiness, where God reigns. A solid crystal floor separates it from chaos, which occupied once all of the other half. When Satan and his angels rebelled against God's newly begotten son,* they were driven through the crystal floor of heaven, and through chaos. During the nine days they were falling through chaos, God's will was creating hell for their reception, at the other side of the infinite sphere, and as far as possible "from God and light and heaven." Hell had a

---

* See "Paradise Lost," Book V, lines 603 and 604.

lake of fire in the center, and it was surrounded by land that burned with solid fire. Outside of this was the frozen continent. Into this dungeon the rebels were shut. Nine days they lay wallowing in the lake of fire, and during these nine days, God was making the starry universe out of the part of chaos that was nearest to the center of the crystal floor of heaven. In the center of the starry universe he places our earth.

We see then that Milton's astronomical scheme is superior to Dante's. But alas! his God has the same terrible features as Dante's God, and both these great poets accepted the eternal abode of torture that they had learned to believe in as members of the Christian church.

Milton's notion of the spirit-world is open to the same objection as Dante's. He makes it all for God, angels, demons, and inhabitants of this world. They both leave wholly out of account the inhabitants of all the other worlds. In comparison with these other worlds, our earth is as one little drop to the Pacific ocean, and no view of the Spirit-world of our earth can be true, unless it be in harmony with the general plan of the universe, and unless it account for all the facts therein.

Friends, it was claimed by the founders of Christianity that the Nazarene was the logos of God. As the Greek word logos means word, this claim means that by Jesus, God spoke to man. So he did, for he

told men that God was spirit, and he forced his followers to believe that life continues after the death
of the body.   Now, friends, this Greek word logos,
meaning word, that was applied to Jesus, also means
science.   Did you ever count how many of the
sciences of our day have the termination logy, which
of course is derived from this very word logos?
Perhaps a hundred sciences end in this same Greek
word, as geology, philology, conchology, astrology,
psychology, demonology, physiology.   What does
this mean?   We think it means simply this.   Long
ago, when Jesus lived, and man was just emerging
from a physical condition, he was taught the spiritual nature of himself and of God.   At that time he
knew but little of the laws of nature.   Jesus
knew how to apply natural forces, but the ignorant
people who surrounded him called his acts miraculous.   But in our age, since Bacon taught us to investigate the forces of nature, in order to use them,
and thus paved the way for all the modern sciences,
it is by the sciences that God speaks to man.   In this
nineteenth century, therefore, the Christ of the age,
in other words the manifestation of Deity, is in all
these various sciences, or "logies," many of which
Bacon foresaw in his "Prodromi."

It is to the test of scientific truth that we now
bring every statement.   To this test we now apply,
not only the material things we see and feel, but the
immaterial substances, as psyche and spirit.   Is

communication by electricity claimed to be possible?
We apply to it the test of science. Is it claimed
that the disembodied can communicate with us by
the application of the laws of magnetism? We apply the test of science. Is it claimed that spirits can
temporarily materialize a physical body? We apply
the test of science. Thus we find that even the
Spirit-world is expected to be in harmony with
what is already scientifically known of this earth as
a member of the solar system.

When the Apostle John lived on the earth, and
when Dante wrote his poem, astronomical notions
were so erroneous that it would have been impossible for them to give a scientific locality to the
Spirit-world. But since astronomy has been put on
the right foundation, since its data have been proved
by the invention of telescopes, and especially since
spirits have been enabled to communicate what they
know to us in the flesh, it has become possible for
us to get a clear notion of the locality of the Spirit-
world. To present this will be the scope of the
remainder of the lecture.

In the first place, let us rid ourselves of the notion that the Spirit-world is disconnected with this
earth on which we now dwell. Let us cast aside
the notion that there is one enormous Spirit-world,
which is the home of all the spirits from all the
worlds in space. This physical earth is our original
home. Here we came into individual existence.

Here we had our experience in physical conditions. This earth is our home now; and by and by, when we leave the physical body, it will be in the spirit-world which belongs to our dear mother earth that we shall dwell. Of course a time may come in the remote future that we may visit other worlds. But in our opinion, that will not be until we shall have advanced so far in spiritual development that it will not be possible for us to communicate with those who will then be living on the surface of the earth in physical conditions. This explains why spirits do not tell us very definitely about life in the other worlds. Meanwhile, let us not expect to know all now, and let us rejoice that we shall have an eternity in which to go on learning of all the aspects of immortal life.

Now to show where the spirit-world of our dear earth is, and to show that it is amply large enough for all that have ever lived on this globe, and for all that will ever live here, we will refer to the simple facts of astronomy. Of course, our spirit-world must be very large—inconceivably large—to make room for all. Geo. A. Schufeldt estimates that at least 177,000,000,000 persons must have lived on the earth, if man began only six thousand years ago. To show ample space for this tremendous number, we offer the following considerations.

This earth seems so very large to us that we generally lose sight of the immense spaces that separate it from the nearest planets. To give us some faint notion of these spaces, let us use an illustration given on page 69 of Steele's " Fourteen Weeks on Astronomy."

We will imagine a large level plain, and in the middle of this plain we will place a globe only two feet in diameter. This globe will represent the sun. We all know that this earth, which seems so large to us, is 8,000 miles in diameter. The diameter of the sun is about 850,000 miles, and it would therefore take more than one hundred earths like our own, strung on a wire, to reach across the sun. It would of course then take more than one million earths like our own, to make up the mass of the sun. In our illustration, however, we represent this enormous mass, equal in bulk to 1,245,000 earths, by the globe two feet in diameter, which we place in the center of our plain to represent the sun. On this scale, Vulcan, the planet nearest to the sun will be about the size of the head of a pin, and yet this minute object will revolve around the sun at the distance of about twenty-seven feet. Mercury will be a mustard seed, and will yet be eighty-two feet from the sun. Venus will be represented by a pea, and it will revolve at a distance of one hundred and forty-two feet. Our great earth, eight thousand miles in diameter, with its continents, Asia, Africa, Europe, North and South America; its great oceans Atlantic, Indian, Pacific, Arctic, and Antarctic, will be represented by another *pea*; and it will perform its revolution around this sun of two feet in diameter, at a distance of *two hundred and fifteen feet*. Mars, the size of a pepper-corn, will be three hundred and twenty-seven feet from the sun. Jupiter, a moderate-sized orange, will be a quarter of a mile distant. Saturn, a small orange, will be two-fifths of a mile away. Uranus, the size of a cherry, will be three-quarters of a mile away. And Neptune, the most distant planet yet discovered, will be represented by a plum, and will perform its revolutions about this globe two feet in diameter, at the distance of one mile and a quarter.

This illustration, clearly conceived by the mind, presents to us one surprising feature. We are amazed by the enormous disproportion existing between the size of the planets and the distance each one is placed from the others and from the central sun. In fact, the thought of a pea, for instance, measuring hour by hour its great orbit, is almost ludicrous. It seems really ridiculous that a plum should perform this enormous revolution, at a distance of one mile and a quarter from its central body. And when we multiply these distances until they reach their true figures, how amazing it is to think that lonely Neptune is measuring his enormous orbit at a distance of 2,800,000,000 miles from the sun! And what a wondrous fact that Venus, our nearest neighbor, excepting our dear own moon, has an orbit about 25,000,000 of miles from our own; while Mars, our nearest neighbor on the outside, never comes nearer to us than does Venus.

Friends, if these worlds that shine in space by the reflected light of the sun, were only the physical worlds that we see with these physical eyes, we might well inquire, "Why are all these enormous empty spaces between this worlds?" and, "Why does all this space run to waste?"

But learning what we have in the last forty years of the condition of those who have left the body, knowing that they can at times revisit us, and that their spirit world is closely allied to our own, what conclusion do we inevitably reach? Is it not reasonable, and in perfect harmony with astronomical science, that the spirit-world of each planet envelops it, and extends away out into the ethereal space, and ever accompanies it, in its stupendous journey around the sun? In accordance with this teaching of our spirit friends, each inhabitant begins existence on its own globe, has his own physical experience there, in time leaves the body, and enters the spirit world contiguous to his own globe. There he finds those he used to know. For a period, he remains in the border-land between the physical world and the spirit-world. As he progresses, he becomes more freed from physical conditions, and passes further on in his own spirit-world.

Where then is the spirit-world of the earth? Is

the physical earth itself a part of the spirit-world? Most certainly. The proof of this lies in the fact that we are spirits, though our spirits are yet confined in the enswathing fleshy covering. Being wrapped in flesh, we are heavier than the air, and are held down to the surface of the earth by a pressure of fifteen pounds to the square inch.

By and by, when we are born the second time, our spiritual body will be born out of this physical body. That spiritual body is lighter than the air, though it has its own ethereal substance. Being freed from the heavy flesh body, it will walk on the air, and naturally ascend to the regions beyond the dense atmosphere which is now our vital breath. We shall feel natural there. We shall feel alive. And when we become used to the means of locomotion, and to the mode of living, we shall find ourselves far better off than while we were going through our physical experience here.

Do you think we shall forget our friends who will be still down on the earth? Indeed we shall not forget them. We shall learn the laws by which we can reach them, and communicate to them the blessed truth that none of us will never die. We shall help them all we can, and prepare a home for them when they too will in their turn drop the conditions of physical life, and enter the beautiful Spirit-world which envelops what we shall always remember as our dear Mother-Earth.

THE BETTER LAND.

" 'I hear thee speak of a better land;
  Thou call'st its children a happy band;
  Mother! Oh, where is that radiant shore,—
  Shall we not seek it and weep no more?
  Is it where the flower of the orange blows,
  And the fire-flies dance through the myrtle boughs?'
      'Not there, not there, my child.'

' Is it where the feathery palm-trees rise,
  And the date grows ripe under sunny skies,
  Or 'midst the green isles of glittering seas,
  Where fragrant forests perfume the breeze,
  And strange bright birds, on their starry wings,
  Bear the rich hues of all glorious things?'
      'Not there, not there, my child.'

' Is it far away in some region old,
  Where the rivers wander o'er sands of gold—
  Where the burning rays of the ruby shine,
  And the diamond lights up the secret mine,
  And the pearl gleams forth from the coral strand,
  Is it there, sweet mother, that better land?'
      'Not there, not there, my child.'

' Eye hath not seen it, my gentle boy!
  Ear hath not heard its deep songs of joy,
  Dreams cannot picture a world so fair,
  Sorrow and death may not enter there;
  Time doth not breath on its fadeless bloom:
  For beyond the clouds and beyond the tomb,
      It is there, it is there, my child.' "

—MRS. HEMANS.

LECTURE XII.

It is sometimes laid to the charge of Spiritualists
that they have no religion, and that they do not
want any. We admit that there are such in our
ranks, but they take this ground because some part
of their nature is yet undeveloped. They are Spiritualists of a low order, and they receive influences
from decarnated ones who still linger in the border
land between the physical and the spiritual world.
Such persons still rest in the phenomena. Provided
they can go to séances, get raps and table-tipping,
get good slate-writing, see persons under control,
and talk with materialized forms, they are perfectly
satisfied. Spiritualism with them consists wholly of
these phenomenal manifestations.

The phenomena certainly form the basis of our
knowledge, for it is these tangible facts that prove
the continuance of life and the return of spirits.
Never shall we weary of receiving tokens of the
love of our departed friends for us. Glad shall we
always be to attend séances and glean information
regarding spirit life, and receive messages of love
and cheer from our dear ones who have been "born

into that undying life." Gladder still are we if in
solitude we be so favored as to hear the tiny tap
and spirit voices, and see our angels hovering near.
Without these phenomena, we should not be *sure*
of spirit, just as Mary Magdalene was not *sure* that
Jesus was alive, until she saw him herself in the
morning twilight in Joseph's garden. But the phenomena, if they lead us to nothing higher, are not
in themselves fitted to unfold our souls. If the
basic facts on which Spiritualism rests do not become incentives to higher spiritual life, they are not
really useful to our future existence. The phenomena form the basis of the fair structure of our philosophy. And all through the facts and the philosophy should be the religion of Spiritualism.

Some of us say, "No religion for me! I have
had enough!" With regard to some applications of
the term religion, we too say the same. We too
have had quite enough of what some persons call
religion. But we take issue, at outset, with all
those who declare that they do not want any religion. We speak on this occasion for those who
want a religion, who discard that kind taught in the
churches, and wish to ponder on the main features
of the religion of the future, the one that will in
time be adopted by all the human race.

Religion in its essence is something that links us
with that which is higher than ourselves, with the
aim of elevating our nature.

The church says that we are fallen, lost, undone; and that religion will save us from sinking into ever-lasting destruction. We have before us the New England Primer, and will give a few extracts found therein from "Spiritual Milk for American babes, drawn out of the breasts of both Testaments for their souls' nourishment."

Q. What hath God done for you?

A. God hath made me, he keepeth me, and he can save me.

Q. How did God make you?

A. In my first parents, holy and righteous.

Q. Are you then born holy and righteous?

A. No, my first father sinned, and I in him.

Q. Are you then born a sinner?

A. I was conceived in sin, and born in iniquity.

Q. What is your birth sin?

A. Adam's sin imputed to me, and a corrupt nature dwelling in me.

Q. How then look you to be saved?

A. Only by Jesus Christ.

Q. How are you the nearer to Christ?

A. As I come to feel my cursed state and need of a Savior.

On such teachings were our ancestors nourished. That the church has been forced the last twenty-five years to modify the extreme views given above is wholly due to communications made by disem-bodied spirits. These messages have penetrated the tight joints of the old theologic armor. Thinking men and women reject the old views quoted above. They refuse to believe that an infinitely powerful being made us so that we inevitably fell "in our first parents," so that from being good, we became wicked. They refuse to believe that this infinite being then planned a way to undo his own work, and by the death of his only son contrived to bring us up again, provided we were willing to appropriate the goodness of that son to ourselves, instead of being good on our own account. They refuse to believe that

"Nothing either great or small
Remains for us to do. "

The religion of the future will have no such unreasonable, pernicious, and immoral features. The whole doctrine of "salvation" and "grace" is unbefitting an omnipotent and beneficent being, who knew what he was about in creating mankind. What! can a creature of God be *lost?* How can he possibly be lost, and that forever? The clergy claim that we need salvation. What do we need to be saved from? From God, who made us?

We are reminded of an incident related by Jenny B. Hagan. An Indian astray on the prairie met some white men. They said to him, "Poor Indian has lost his way." Straightening himself up with all the dignity of a sachem, he said, "No: *Indian* not lost. *Wigwam* lost!"

Friends, progression is a better thing than re-
demption or salvation; development is better than
fall; and continued and ever advancing life is better
than resurrection.

The "religion" doled out to "American babes" in
the last century is a sort that a reasonable man, who
thinks without shackles, does not receive.

Such a religion has been taught for many hundred
years, and it was claimed that the heathen must
accept it or be damned.   To-day the heathen world
is increasing in numbers much faster than conver-
sions to Christainity are made.   Moreover, in Christian lands the number of persons who become either
Spiritualists or materialists each year is larger than
the number of persons who join the "orthodox"
churches in the same period of time.   Heathen nations do not adopt the scheme of religion above described, and millions in Christendom are discarding
it as unjust and foolish.

Some other form of religion than that called
Christianity is what mankind will want in the long
run.   When we say Christainity, of course we
mean the system taught by the churches.   We do
not mean what Jesus really taught.   Though spirits
now have progressed in some respects further than
he did, he really taught pure Spiritualism; and his
teachings directly rested, as do ours, on spiritual
manifestations. *He* taught that God is our father,
that all men are brethren, that we must cultivate

perfection of nature to the heart's core, and that we shall stand or fall according as we act here. He was sufficiently tinctured with the old Judaic views to make the mistake of believing in eternal punishment, and he did not see clearly the infinite progression that will sometime become the law of life for all souls. His doctrines of morality, like those of Buddha, are unexceptionable. But the views of both Buddha and Jesus are inferior to the views revealed by the new and glorious light of Spiritualism.

Buddha's future state amounts to annihilation. Memory disappears with each new so-called incarnation, and conscious individuality is everlastingly submerged, as the Buddhistic soul is absorbed in Nirvana. Spiritualists know that our individuality, once realized, is consciously preserved through all development. Jesus taught eternal punishment for some. We Spiritualists know that suffering will cease when it has done its purifying work, and that progression will be the happy lot of all.

As was said before, the Christianity that has been taught by the churches is not acceptable to the mass of mankind, and it cannot be forced upon them. A standing problem with the clergy is how to regain the prestige once possessed. How to get people to attend church is the great question. Little by little has the church slipped from its old moorings. But the mass of mankind have gone too fast for it, and it will continue to be so. Ecclesiastical power cannot preserve the authority it craves without some holding-point, as a creed, or a sacred book. No doubt they will try to keep a following. If there be no other way to keep it, the church may try to seize Spiritualism itself, and try to formulate it by a creed, and legislate for it by a synod, and prescribe for it by sacred writings. But we need suffer no second bondage in this age of the world. The rise of ecclesiastical power after the time of Christ was founded on two erroneous claims. One of these claims was that the spiritual manifestations produced by Jesus and his followers were miracles, and effected by supernatural power. The other erroneous claim was that the Bible was inspired by Almighty God, and therefore infallible. Adhering closely to these two points, priests were able to control Christendom. Thus did they dominate over human reason, and bring the Dark Ages onto Europe.

As the church becomes more and more convinced that the claims of Spiritualism are true, it will try to get control of it, and use it as an engine for tyrannizing over human reason. But, if Spiritualists are true to its principles, they will not be able to accomplish this subjugation. The reasons are manifold, and we will point out some of them.

In the first place, the laws of Nature are now understood far better than they were at the beginning of the Christian era. Jesus did what he did in accordance with Nature's laws. Men, not understanding this, thought his deeds were miracles. The communications of the spirit world being made by the application of the laws of science by skilled spirits, these manifestations are not miraculous; and designing priests cannot make use of them to control mankind. All can form circles, and if they do it in accordance with spiritual laws, they can develop mediums, and communicate with the disembodied for themselves. The spirit world is working to lead the whole human race into that spiritual era when all can communicate freely with their friends who have passed into the life beyond.

Again, the advance of the principles of Spiritualism will show the world that new and greater messages are constantly given to us by decarnated spirits, who are themselves learning all the time. Under their wise tuition, many have already learned, and all will sometime learn, that new truths will be revealed to us as long as existence shall continue; and that the claim of a Bible completed hundreds of years ago is an obstacle to human progress. The principles of Spiritualism also teach us that a formulated creed is a wrong and a useless thing. What is believed in one age of the world will be discarded by a succeeding age, provided that mankind progress. Away with all cast-iron moulds!

> " We must upward still, and onward,
> Who would keep abreast of Truth."

So, friends, though the church itself should after

a time try to appropriate Spiritualism, and try to use her as an instrument to bind the human soul in chains, she will find it impossible to do so, if we remember how she has done it in times past, and guard against such methods in the future. By uniting with the Spirit world in applying the laws of Nature to a more general communication between the two worlds, we can prevent ecclesiasts from ruling the world by so-called miracles. By ever holding in view the truth that new and grander knowledge is constantly coming to us from advancing spirits, we can prevent dogmatists from hampering mankind by stereotyped Bibles and formulated creeds.

Let us adhere closely to the main elements of spiritual freedom. What are those elements? They are the use of our individual reason, the acceptance of personal instruction from advanced disembodied spirits, and a determination to guide our own conduct by the laws that govern the progression of the spirit in endless duration. As man becomes more spiritual, more and more persons can communicate for themselves with the other world, and drink individually from those fountains of true freedom. The shackles of creed and force will fall away, and he will, while here below, possess the truth that will make him free indeed.

Let us now consider some of the features of the religion that accords with the higher phases of Spiritualism, and show it to be reasonable, adapted

to the needs of the human race, and harmonious
with a proper view of the infinite spirit.

What is the origin of the religion of Spiritualism?
It originated like all others in spiritual manifestations.
But it has one great advantage over all the rest.
While others rest on phenomena that took place
long, long ago, and have to be taken on testimony;
its manifestations are recent and present, and can be
tested by all who will take the trouble to test them.
Spiritualism is not founded, like Christianity, on
phenomena that took place 1900 years ago; like
Mohammedanism, on manifestations 1270 years
gone by; like Judaism, on prophesies and so-called
miracles, 2,000 to 4,000 years ago. Unlike all
these, its solid foundation is in manifestations made
daily and hourly in enlightened and scientific nations.
Our nation would smile at the thought of accepting
a religion just originating among a people as unenlightened as the Arabs in the time of Mohammed, or
the Jews in the time of Herod or Abraham. We
are not called to do so. The religion we advocate
has its origin in the best thought of our age, and it
has elements that will enable it to keep abreast with
all succeeding and advancing ages.

This religion harmonizes with science, instead of
contradicting it, as did the Christianity of the Dark
Ages. Its phenomena are founded on laws of
physical and spiritual science that we are just beginning to understand, and that scientific spirits like

Faraday and John King are applying with more
and more skill with each revolving year.   Raps and
table tippings are produced by the application of
the laws of magnetism.   Spirit telegraphy is used
to communicate thought by disembodied operators
who understand how to use electric forces.   Celestial chemists have learned to give us photographs
of the spiritual body; to write between closed slates;
to disintegrate flowers in green-houses, and re-make
them from their elements between closed slates;
and, more surprising still, to make temporary forms
from certain elements drawn from the entranced
body of a medium, that can walk and talk and dematerialize while inhabited by a disembodied spirit.
Spirit physicians, aided by bands of trained atten-
dants, cure diseases of the mortal body, and also
"minister to the mind diseased."   We are just beginning to find out what can be done by the spirit-
world.   Each year brings new phases of manifestation, and the most inspired of mortals would be surprised if brought face to face with the phenomena
of fifty years to come.   Let us do our part, and
earnestly aid decarnated beings to prove to mortals
that the soul does survive the death of the body,
and that spirit is the real substance, of which this
material world is only the shadow.

Our religion is philosphical, as well as scientific,
which is more than can be said of orthodoxy.   Philosophy demands that each effect must have its cause,

in accordance with the laws of nature.   It demands that acts shall produce their legitimate effects. Good acts shall produce advancement, *per se*—and not because the doer subscribes to some theological dogma.   Evil acts shall produce ill effects, in spite of a person's having laid that evil act on the person of Jesus.   Spiritualism philosophically teaches that violations of the laws of nature will hinder our progression, and that living in accordance with the laws of nature will further our progression, no matter what religious dogmas we accept or reject, no matter whether we be Buddhists, or Spiritualists, or Baptists.   Spiritualism is thoroughly natural.   It discards all miracles, and all supernaturalism.   It shows us that we shall feel just as natural out of the body as in the body, and that we shall be just as subject to the laws of Nature *there* as *here*.

The true religion gives a view of God that is far superior to that adopted by the Church.   The god of Judaism was wrathful, revengeful, and partial. Calvin's god had to be propitiated, because he had constructed us in such a way that we fell like Adam and Eve, or had the sins of Adam and Eve imputed to us, besides our own.   Spiritualists believe in infinite life, that infinite life in motion gives the laws of nature, and that all the products of infinite life are destined to progress forever.   They believe that the germs of individual being are originally good, because they are the offspring of infinite life;

that those germs are obliged, by the laws of their being, to develop as fast as their circumstances will allow, and that this development will go on more rapidly and more blissfully as the ages roll on.

What is the chief end of man, according to Spiritualism? Man's chief end is to find out the laws of the universe in which he finds himself an individuality, and to adapt himself to those laws, so that he may lay the foundation of progression here, and go on progressing forever and ever.

Spiritualism is adapted to our present state, because it teaches us to obey the laws of physical development. It tells us to keep our bodies clean, pure, temperate, and a fit temple for our spiritual body. Our immortal part is temporarily enshrined in this physical form, and if we develop it here by right actions, we shall not enter spirit life in a crippled condition.

The true religion is good for us intellectually, because it frees us from all prejudice, and thus enables us to receive pure truth from those whose greater knowledge fits them to be our teachers. It is reasonable, philosophical, and natural, and has progression as its object. For these reasons, it satisfies us; and we find that the further we go, the more satisfactory does it become.

It satisfies the heart, as well as the physical and the intellectual nature. Instead of teaching us that members of a family will be separated forever, because they differed in regard to some theological doctrine, it proves to us that those who love each other will be together in the sweet by and by. Instead of trying to make us accept the notion that hundreds of millions will be swept into eternal perdition because they did not "accept the righteousness" of somebody of whom they never heard, it shows us that the Chinese, the American Indians, the Abyssinians, in fact all men, of whatever race, or age, or nation, will have a chance to progress in the next life. The poor Hottentot, who prays devoutly to his fetish, and loves his wife and child, will according to its teachings enter spirit life on a brighter plane than the "Christian" capitalist who grinds money out of the poor; than the married tyrant who allows his conjugal slave to commit murder by making conception abortive, so that he may gratify his physical lust; than the clergyman who veils a lascivious heart by the robe of sanctity: or a physician who misuses his skill, by murdering an unborn babe at the request of its unnatural parents.

Persons whose reason dominates the body engage in the sexual act with a view to procreate offspring. And as all beings begin existence on the physical plane, such acts belong only to physical existence. Persons who find their chief pleasure in the indulgence of sensual gratifications will find themselves unable to progress in spirit life, until they have rid themselves of that condition.

Spiritualism teaches humanity. It tells us to be kind to our dumb animals, our beasts of burden, and our pets, because if we fail to show loving care to beings who are dependent on us, we are hindering the development of our own souls. It rebukes the pride of women who allow their horses' heads to be held up by the cruel overcheck rein, in order to satisfy their own vanity; and the cruelty of men who maim their animals by docking their tails—because it is the fashion!

It sternly condemns those who practice vivisection on harmless animals, except in rare and extreme cases where one competent surgeon is actually finding out some definite fact that may lessen the suffering of many. That vivisection be practised in order to instruct a class of students, or to gratify the curiosity of savants is outrageous in the extreme. In all cases, anæsthetics should be administered, and the animal killed before regaining consciousness. Is science intended to brutalize human beings? The tendency of true science is to make us more humane, and more thoughtful for those who are weaker than ourselves.

Especially does our religion teach us to be humane to little children. They should be welcomed into existence, and the principles of spiritual progression should be instilled into their souls by the authors of their being. Spiritualism goes to the root of the family system, and seeks to prevent marriages that

are not founded on a mutual love and friendship between a man and woman which began in their noblest and most spiritual hours. Such a marriage
will not result in the murder of unborn children, and
in the strife between husband and wife which harms
the moral nature of their little ones.

We believe that all individual spirits, in all worlds,
began their existence on the physical plane. They
were individualized from the infinite spirit in the
physical body of their parent. Conception, gesta-
tion, and birth from the body of the mother, attend
the beginning of our personal existence on this earth.
These acts do not then take place in the Spirit-world.
They have no place there, for existence does not begin there. But, to the Spiritualist, these acts are
fraught with a dignity and an importance that rests
on his knowledge that the life here begun will continue forever and will eternally progress.

True marriage, between a good man and a good
woman, who know that they are pro-creating a being destined to eternal advancement, is a noble and
a blessed thing. The union being one in which the
conjugal affections are directed to but one person,
the choice being reciprocal, free, for life, and pub-
licly ratified,* we have the origin of the family. In
this way only can the different family relations be
clearly defined. A family, thus begun, will continue

---

* See page 247 of "A System of Moral Science," by Drs. Hickok and
Seelye.

its relations in the Spirit-world.   And even where the family relation fails to reach ideal perfection, it will still continue.   The parents will love their children, the children will love their parents, relations will be interested in each other, and friendship will continue, just so long as we shall remember our life in this world, and so long as we continue to cherish love for dear Mother Earth, where we *began to be*.

As to Theosophy, it rests on theory, while Spiritualism rests on facts; those decarnated spirits who adopt it, take it theoretically and give no proof of it; some who passed to the other side of life long before the time of Moses know nothing of it; it takes away all consciousness of individuality by nullifying the memory—memory being the only proof of identity.   Theosophy, in short, contradicts the facts of Spiritualism by dogmatic assumption; and it subverts the principles of Spiritualism, especially that basic and most glorious principle—conscious individuality, and conscious progression.   As Mrs. R. S. Lillie lately remarked, Spiritualists who try to ride at one and the same time on the three horses — Spiritualism, Theosophy, and Christian Science — will not be able to maintain a very firm seat.

This religion teaches us to be true.   By and by when out of the body we must be true, because deceit can exist only under physical conditions.   If false here, we shall not be happy there till we have learned to take pleasure in being true.

Spiritualism teaches absolute and universal love and helpfulness, without bounds and without an end. We shall not get on there, if we do not try to help all whom we can help. Advanced spirits stretch tender, helpful hands down to those on a lower plane; they aspire with admiration and docility to those who have attained a greater height than their own.

Becoming conscious that eternal progression is the object for which we were created, our life on earth is ennobled. Death loses all its terrors, for it is a garlanded gateway into a nobler life. Our heart swells as we get faint glimpses of the heights that humanity is destined to attain. Some have these glorious thoughts and hopes, but they keep them shut up in their own breasts, for fear of offending the prejudices of society. Ah! friends, let us lay by all such fears, and give these joyous hopes to all with whom we come in contact. Let us use every possible means to strengthen each other, and to bind in a helpful band all those who see the light upon the mountain tops.

Church organization riveted the fetters of the human mind so fast, that some of us are afraid to organize in any way. Certainly we shall never subscribe to any form that can hinder progress. It is dangerous to formulate what we now believe, because by and by new information may lead us to believe quite differently.   But, if we are Spiritualists, there are certain things that we *know*.   We KNOW that the spirit survives the death of the physical body, and that there *is* intelligent communication between the living and the so-called dead.   We also *know* that progression is the law of existence, both now and hereafter.   As Progressive Spiritualists, we accept all true spiritual manifestations as being direct proofs of the continuity of life; and we desire by works of humanity, truth, and love, to develop ourselves while on the earth plane, so that our advancement may be more rapid, after we leave the physical body.

We want no creed, for a creed soon wears out or grows too tight, and has to be cast off by a live, growing body.   But it seems to us that there are certain things that all Spiritualists know, that they reach after, and that this knowledge and these aspirations may readily form a basis of union that will cause Spiritualism to reach more souls, and do more effective work for all humanity, both in the body and out of the body.   For my part, I expect to be a Progressive Spiritualist, both "now and never so many myriads of ages hence."

A DREAM OF HEAVEN.

FROM A LONDON NEWSPAPER.

"Lo! the seal of Death is breaking;
  Those who slept its sleep are waking;
    Eden opes her portals fair:
  Hark! the harps of joy are ringing;
  Hark! the seraph hymn is singing,
  And the living rills are flinging
    Music on immortal air.

"There, no more at eve declining,
  Suns without a cloud are shining,
    O'er the land of life and love.
  Heaven's own harvest woos the reaper,
  Heaven's own dreams entrance the sleeper,
  Not a tear is left the weeper,
    To profane one flower above.

"No frail lilies there are breathing,
  There no thorny rose is wreathing,
    In the bowers of Paradise,
  Where the founts of life are flowing,
  Flowers unknown to earth are blowing,
  Mid superber verdure glowing,
    Than is sunned by mortal skies.

" There the groves of heaven, that never
　Fade or fall, are green forever,
　　Mirrored in the radiant tide.
There along the sacred waters,
Unprofaned by tears or slaughters,
Wander earth's immortal daughters,
　　And shall evermore abide.

" There no sigh of memory swelleth,
　There no tear of misery dwelleth,
　　Hearts will bleed or break no more.
Past is all the cold world's scorning,　·
Gone the night and broke the morning,
With seraphic day adorning
　　Life's glad wave and golden shore.

" Oh! on that bright shore to wander,
　Trace those radiant waves' meander,
　　All we loved and lost to see!
Is this thought, so pure, so splendid,
Vainly with our being blended?
No! with time ye are not ended,
　　Visions of eternity."

PERSONAL COMMUNICATIONS.

The following communications were given to the writer of this book, under circumstances that make their authenticity indisputable. They were given in connection with my questions and remarks, by an "independent slate writer." Some were written in my lap on the inside of a slate from which I had just rubbed out the previous communication. I had closed the slate and then I held it shut fast with both my hands in my lap. I heard and felt the writing, opened it myself, read it, and copied it on the spot. *Strange?* Yes: *but true.* It was a bright morning, the curtains were wide open, and the room as light as the sun could make it.

Given Aagust 26, 1890.

"I am glad to come to you.

ADONIRAM JUDSON."

"I come to my love. MOTHER."

Given August 27, 1890.

"How best to unfold the soul is the question. I am anxious Edward should enjoy this truth. The spirit of benevolence and truth is his.

Your father, ADONIRAM JUDSON."

I had been remarking that I had learned that his first wife, Mrs. Ann H. Judson, is nearest to him in spirit life, and I was querying whether my own mother had found a soul mate, when this was written:

"Dear child, in spirit I come, and watch over my children.   I am as yet in oneness with them.

MOTHER."

I asked father who the man was with benignant, intellectual face, whose head is close to my brain in my spirit photograph.   He said:

"You did not know him in life. It was Edwards."

Further inquiry elicited the fact that it was the author of the "Freedom of the Will."   I expressed my surprise that one like him should come to me, though I had been strongly interested in his character for many years.   Father replied:

"Surely, Jonathan Edwards. You had a drawing, because he was near you."

Then came the following communication:

"Dear friend, my mission to earth was to enlighten the world.   You have taught in your way.   You are called to a higher school.   EDWARDS."

Remarking that timidity and a weak voice were in the way of my doing public work, he said:

"Yes, child; you will speak and write.

EDWARDS."

"What," said I, shall I get up and face an audience, when I do not know what I am going to say?"

"We will fill your mouth," was his reply.

I ask myself why one with so powerful an intellect and so exalted a character should aid one so inferior as myself. It can only be accounted for by the fact that I have a strong sympathy with and liking for his mind and character. It is as if a poor little autoharp were placed beside a Chickering or Steinway grand piano. The inferior instrument vibrates in unison with the magnificent chords drawn from the mighty one.

Given August 29, 1890.

"My daughter, we are blest to have this meeting. It takes away the pain of parting.   MOTHER."

"And I am here with mother, dear child. Bless you.   AUNTY WADE."

"My beautiful boys! I am proud of them. I am glad they are leading the people, but I wish they would speak more understandingly of God's great love.   MOTHER."

"I want to speak to you of this new work of yours. We cannot make others come into our light until they *grow* there. There are many minds who have been educated in the world's lore, who may be as ignorant as the poor, benighted ones I taught, and who must be taught in the same way, with patience and love.   ADONIRAM."

On my asking him if he had been able to manifest to me at a certain séance, he said:

"There are many pitfalls for you. Think well, and let reason balance the manifestations."

Given August 30, 1890.

"There may be many days before I can talk with you face to face; but soul to soul, like the blending of light, will our souls mingle.   FATHER."

"I want to tell you why I came on that picture. Because I saw in you one who may do a good work with a class of people that others could not.

E. V. WILSON."

"Now, my little girl, I may not write you, but you know that mother's love is a shield and a comfort to you, that mother's lullaby is a sweet song of peace.

MOTHER."

"My student, I too am a student in the expression of truth. We will go on, learning and teaching together.   J. EDWARDS."

(In answer to a question.)

"Yes; the real is not seen. The soul sends out buds that blossom to the external, only in the fulness of things. Go on brave and strong.

Your father, A. J."

Given Feb. 10, 1891.

"Look to the world at large, my dear daughter.

SARAH."

www.ingramcontent.com/pod-product-compliance
Lightning Source LLC
Chambersburg PA
CBHW020052030726
47498CB00006B/1741